JAVA PROGRAMS TO ACCOMPANY PROGRAMMING LOGIC AND DESIGN

by Jo Ann Smith

THOMSON
™
COURSE TECHNOLOGY

Java Programs to Accompany Programming Logic and Design
by Jo Ann Smith

Executive Editor:
Mac Mendelsohn

Senior Product Manager:
Tricia Boyle

Development Editor:
Jill Batistick

Production Editor:
Philippa Lehar

Editorial Assistant:
Amanda Piantedosi

Manufacturing Coordinator:
Laura Burns

Marketing Manager:
Brian Berkeley

Cover Designer:
Nancy Goulet

Compositor:
GEX Publishing Services

■■■■BRIEF CONTENTS

PREFACE   vii

CHAPTER ONE
An Introduction to Java and the Java Programming Environment   1

CHAPTER TWO
Variables, Operators, and Writing Programs Using Sequential Statements   11

CHAPTER THREE
Writing Programs That Make Decisions   27

CHAPTER FOUR
Writing Programs Using Loops   47

CHAPTER FIVE
Writing Control Break Programs and Reading Data from Input Files   69

CHAPTER SIX
Using Arrays in Java Programs   81

CHAPTER SEVEN
Sorting Data and Advanced Array Manipulation   93

CHAPTER EIGHT
Using Menus and Performing Data Validation   107

INDEX   125

■■■■■TABLE OF CONTENTS

PREFACE   vii

CHAPTER ONE
An Introduction to Java and the Java Programming Environment   1
   The Java Programming Language   2
   Three Types of Java Programs   2
   An Introduction to Object-Oriented Terminology   3
   Downloading the Java 2 Platform, Standard Edition (J2SE) Version 1.4.2   3
   The Structure of a Java Program   4
   The Java Development Cycle   6
      Writing Java Source Code   6
      Compiling a Java Program   7
      Executing a Java Program   8
      Exercise 1-1: Understanding Java Utilities   8
      Lab 1-1: Compiling and Executing a Java Program   9

CHAPTER TWO
Variables, Operators, and Writing Programs Using Sequential Statements   11
   Variables   12
      Variable Names   12
      Java Data Types   12
      Exercise 2-1: Using Java Variables, Data Types, and Keywords   13
   Declaring and Initializing Variables   13
      Exercise 2-2: Declaring and Initializing Java Variables   14
      Lab 2-1: Declaring and Initializing Java Variables   15
   Arithmetic and Assignment Operators   15
      Arithmetic Operators   15
      Assignment Operators and the Assignment Statement   16
      Precedence and Associativity   18
      Exercise 2-3: Understanding Operator Precedence and Associativity   18
      Lab 2-2: Working with Arithmetic and Assignment Operators   20
   Java Comments   20
   Sequential Statements   21
      Exercise 2-4: Understanding Sequential Statements   23
      Lab 2-3: Using Sequential Statements in a Java Program   25

CHAPTER THREE
Writing Programs That Make Decisions   27
   Boolean Operators   28
      Relational Operators   28
      Logical Operators   29
   Comparing Strings   30
   Decision Statements   32
      The if Statement   32
      Exercise 3-1: Understanding if Statements   34
      Lab 3-1: Using if Statements   34
      The if else Statement   35
      Exercise 3-2: Understanding if else Statements   36
      Lab 3-2: Using if else Statements   37

Nested if Statements   38
Exercise 3-3: Understanding Nested if Statements   39
Lab 3-3: Using Nested if Statements   40
Using Decision Statements to Make Multiple Comparisons   41
Using AND Logic   41
Using OR Logic   42
Exercise 3-4: Making Multiple Comparisons in Decision Statements   42
Lab 3-4: Making Multiple Comparisons in Decision Statements   44

CHAPTER FOUR
Writing Programs Using Loops   47
The Increment (++) and Decrement (--) Operators   48
Exercise 4-1: Using the Increment and Decrement Operators   49
Writing a while Loop in Java   50
Exercise 4-2: Using a while Loop   51
Using a Counter to Control a Loop   52
Exercise 4-3: Using a Counter-Controlled while Loop   53
Lab 4-1: Using a Counter-Controlled while Loop   53
Using a Sentinel Value to Control a Loop   54
Exercise 4-4: Using a Sentinel Value to Control a while Loop   55
Lab 4-2: Using a Sentinel Value to Control a while Loop   55
Using an Event to Control a Loop   56
Exercise 4-5: Using an Event to Control a while Loop   57
Lab 4-3: Using an Event to Control a while Loop   58
Writing a for Loop in Java   59
Exercise 4-6: Using a for Loop   60
Lab 4-4: Using a for Loop   61
Writing a do while Loop in Java   61
Exercise 4-7: Using a do while Loop   62
Lab 4-5: Using a do while Loop   62
Nesting Loops   63
Exercise 4-8: Nesting Loops   64
Lab 4-6: Nesting Loops   65
Accumulating Totals in a Loop   65
Exercise 4-9: Accumulating Totals in a Loop   67
Lab 4-7: Accumulating Totals in a Loop   68

CHAPTER FIVE
Writing Control Break Programs and Reading Data from Input Files   69
File Input   70
Importing Packages and Classes   70
Opening a File   71
Reading Data from an Input File   71
Reading Data Using a Loop and EOF   72
Exercise 5-1: Opening Files and Performing File Input   72
Lab 5-1: Using an Input File   73
Accumulating Totals in Single-Level Control Break Programs   73
Exercise 5-2: Accumulating Totals in Single-Level Control Break Programs   78
Lab 5-2: Accumulating Totals in Single-Level Control Break Programs   79

CHAPTER SIX
Using Arrays in Java Programs 81
Array Basics 82
   Declaring Arrays 82
   Initializing Arrays 83
   Accessing Array Elements 84
   Staying Within the Bounds of an Array 85
   Exercise 6-1: Working with Array Basics 85
   Lab 6-1: Using Arrays 86
Searching an Array for an Exact Match 86
   Exercise 6-2: Searching an Array for an Exact Match 87
   Lab 6-2: Searching an Array for an Exact Match 88
Parallel Arrays 89
   Exercise 6-3: Using Parallel Arrays 90
   Lab 6-3: Using Parallel Arrays 91

CHAPTER SEVEN
Sorting Data and Advanced Array Manipulation 93
Why Should Data Be Sorted? 94
Swapping Data Values 94
   Exercise 7-1: Swapping Values 95
   Lab 7-1: Swapping Values 95
Using a Bubble Sort 96
   The housekeeping() Module 97
   The sortScores() and switchValues() Modules 99
   The finishUp() Module 101
   Exercise 7-2: Using a Bubble Sort 101
   Lab 7-2: Using a Bubble Sort 102
Multidimensional Arrays 103
   Exercise 7-3: Using Multidimensional Arrays 104
   Lab 7-3: Using Multidimensional Arrays 105

CHAPTER EIGHT
Using Menus and Performing Data Validation 107
The switch Statement 108
   Exercise 8-1: Using a switch Statement 109
   Lab 8-1: Using a switch Statement 110
Writing Menu-Driven Programs in Java 111
   The startUp() Module 112
   The looping() Module 113
   The cleanUp() Module 117
   Exercise 8-2: Using Menu-Driven Programs 117
   Lab 8-2: Menu-Driven Programs. 118
Validating Input 118
   Testing for an Exact Match 119
   Validating a Data Type 119
   Validating a Data Range 121
   Validating Reasonableness and Consistency of Data 123
   Validating the Presence of Data 123
   Exercise 8-3: Validating User Input 123
   Lab 8-3: Validating User Input 124

INDEX 125

■ ■ ■ ■PREFACE

Java Programs to Accompany Programming Logic and Design is designed to provide students with an opportunity to write Java programs as part of an Introductory Programming Logic course. It is written to be a companion text to the student's primary text, *Programming Logic and Design, Third Edition*. This book assumes no programming language experience and provides the beginning programmer with a guide to writing structured programs using introductory elements of the popular Java programming language. It is not intended to be a textbook for a course in Java programming. The writing is non-technical and emphasizes good programming practices. The examples do not assume mathematical background beyond high school math. Additionally, the examples illustrate one or two major points; they do not contain so many features that students become lost following irrelevant and extraneous details.

The examples in *Java Programs to Accompany Programming Logic and Design* are often examples presented in the primary textbook, *Programming Logic and Design, Third Edition*. We are providing the following correlation grid so that you can see how the two books map to each other:

Java Programs to Accompany Programming Logic and Design	Programming Logic and Design, Third Edition
Chapter 1: An Introduction to Java and the Java Programming Environment	Chapters 1–4: 1. An Overview of Computers and Logic 2. Understanding Structure 3. Modules, Hierarchy Charts and Documentation 4. Writing and Designing a Complete Program
Chapter 2: Variables, Operators, and Writing Programs Using Sequential Statements	Chapter 4: Writing and Designing a Complete Program
Chapter 3: Writing Programs That Make Decisions	Chapter 5: Making Decisions
Chapter 4: Writing Programs Using Loops	Chapter 6: Looping
Chapter 5: Writing Control Break Programs and Reading Data from Input Files	Chapter 7: Control Breaks
Chapter 6: Using Arrays in Java Programs	Chapter 8: Arrays
Chapter 7: Sorting Data and Advanced Array Manipulation	Chapter 9: Advanced Array Manipulation (Comprehensive edition only)
Chapter 8: Using Menus and Performing Data Validation	Chapter 10: Using Menus and Validating Input (Comprehensive edition only)

Organization and Coverage

Java Programs to Accompany Programming Logic and Design provides students with a review of the programming concepts they encounter in their primary textbook. It also shows them how to use Java to transform their program logic and design into working programs. The structure of a Java program, how to compile and run a Java program, and introductory object-oriented concepts are introduced in Chapter 1. Chapter 2 discusses Java's data types, variables, arithmetic and assignment operators, and using sequential statements to write a complete Java program. Chapters 3 and 4 introduce students to writing Java programs that make decisions and programs that use looping constructs. Students learn to use Java to develop more sophisticated programs that read data from input files and to use control breaks and arrays in Chapters 5 and 6. In Chapter 7, students learn to sort data items stored in an array and also how to use multi-dimensional arrays in Java. Lastly, in Chapter 8, students learn to use Java to write interactive, menu-driven programs and are also introduced to some of the techniques that allow programmers to validate data that is entered by users as programs run.

This book combines text explanation of concepts and syntax along with pseudocode and actual Java code examples to provide students with the knowledge they need to implement their logic and program designs using the Java programming language. This book provides paper and pencil exercises as well as lab exercises after each major topic is introduced. The exercises provide students with experience in reading and writing Java code as well as modifying and debugging existing code. In the labs, students are asked to complete partially prewritten Java programs. Using partially prewritten programs allows students to focus on individual concepts rather than an entire program. The labs also allow students the opportunity to see their programs execute.

Java Programs to Accompany Programming Logic and Design is unique because of the following:

- It is written and designed to correspond to the topics in students' primary textbook, *Programming Language and Design, Third Edition.*
- The examples are everyday examples; no specific knowledge of mathematics, accounting, or other disciplines is assumed.
- It is written to introduce students to introductory elements of the Java programming language, rather than serving to overwhelm beginning programmers with more detail than they are prepared to use or understand.
- Text explanation is interspersed with pseudocode from their primary book so that students are familiar with the presented logic.
- Complex programs are built through the use of complete business examples. Students see how an application is built from start to finish instead of studying only segments of programs.

Features of the Text

Every chapter in this book includes the following features. These features are conducive to learning in the classroom and enable students to learn the material at their own pace.

- Objectives: Each chapter begins with a list of objectives so that the student knows the topics that will be presented within it. In addition to providing a quick reference to topics covered, this feature serves as a useful study aid.
- Figures and illustrations: This book has plenty of visuals, which provide the reader with a more complete learning experience rather than one that involves simply studying text.

TIP □ □ □ □

- Tips: These notes provide additional information—for example, common errors to recognize and avoid.

- Exercises: Each section of each chapter includes meaningful paper and pencil exercises that allow students to practice the skills and concepts they are learning in the section.

- Labs: Each section of each chapter offers meaningful lab work that allows students to write and execute programs that implement their logic and program design.

Acknowledgments

I would like to thank all of the people who helped to make this book possible, especially Jill Batistick, Development Editor, who offered me encouragement, patience, humor, and flexibility when I needed it. Her expertise, hard work, and attention to detail have made this a better textbook. Thanks also to Tricia Boyle, Senior Product Manager; Mac Mendelsohn, Executive Editor; Phillipa Lehar, Production Editor; and Burt LaFontaine, Quality Assurance Tester. It is a pleasure to work with so many fine people who are dedicated to producing quality instructional materials.

I am grateful to the many reviewers who provided helpful and insightful comments during the development of this book, including R. Scott Cost, University of Maryland—Baltimore County; Anne Nelson, High Point University; and Pam Silvers, Asheville-Buncombe Technical Community College.

I am dedicating this book to my husband, Ray. He is my constant source of support in whatever project I happen to undertake.

Jo Ann Smith

■ ■ ■ ■READ THIS BEFORE YOU BEGIN

TO THE USER

Data Files

To complete most of the labs, you will need data files that have been created for this book. Your instructor will provide the data files to you. You also can obtain the files electronically from the Course Technology Web site by connecting to **www.course.com**, and then searching for this book title.

You can use a computer in your school lab or your own computer to complete the labs in this book.

Solutions

Solutions to labs and exercises are provided to instructors on the Course Technology Web site at **www.course.com**. The solutions are password protected.

Using Your Own Computer

To use your own computer to complete the material in this textbook, you will need the following:

- A Pentium 166MHz or faster processor running Microsoft Windows XP, 2000, 98, NT 4.0, or ME with at least 32 megabytes of physical RAM. This book was written using Microsoft Windows ME and quality assurance tested using Microsoft Windows XP. 371 MB or more of free disk space is required for a full install.
- Sun Java 2 SDK Standard Edition version 1.4.1 or 1.4.2.

Downloading the J2SE for the Windows Platform

To download the J2SE, go to the J2SE Web site at **http://java.sun.com/j2se/1.4.2/download.html**. Scroll down to the label "Download J2SE v 1.4.2_0x," where x represents the latest release. Under the SDK column, click the link to download, which should be to the right of "32-bit/64-bit for Windows/Linux/Solaris SPARC," and then follow the on-screen instructions. **Note: These instructions may change as Sun updates their Web site and/or the download procedure.**

Installing the J2SDK

To run the Java 2 SDK Installation Program, double-click the downloaded file, and then follow the on-screen instructions.

Temporarily Updating Your PATH Environment Variable

1. Go to the command prompt.
2. Type the following: *PATH=%PATH%;drive:\ pathname\bin*, where *drive* is the drive letter that contains your SDK installation and *pathname* is the complete pathname of the SDK folder. For example, your command might be *PATH=%PATH%;C:\j2sdk1.4.2_04\bin* if your installation is on drive C in the j2sdk1.4.2_04 folder.

3. Press **Enter**. Now you can compile Java programs from any folder on your system. This command must be typed in each time you open a DOS console window to compile or execute a Java program.

Temporarily Updating Your CLASSPATH Environment Variable

1. Go to the command prompt.
2. Type the following: **set CLASSPATH=%CLASSPATH%;.** Note that the . (period) after the ; (semicolon) must be typed.
3. Press **Enter**.

TO THE INSTRUCTOR

Solutions to labs and exercises are provided to instructors on the Course Technology Web site at **www.course.com**. The solutions are password protected.

To complete some of the exercises and labs in this book, your students must use a set of data files. These files are available on the Course Technology Web site at **www.course.com**. Follow the instructions in the Help file to copy the data files to your server or standalone computer. You can view the Help file using a text editor such as WordPad or Notepad. Once the files are copied, you may instruct your students how to copy the files to their own computers or workstations.

Course Technology Data Files

You are granted a license to copy the data files to any computer or computer network used by individuals who have purchased this book.

1

AN INTRODUCTION TO JAVA AND THE JAVA PROGRAMMING ENVIRONMENT

After studying Chapter 1, you will be able to:

- [ ] Understand the Java programming language and its history
- [ ] Recognize the three types of Java programs
- [ ] Understand introductory concepts and terminology used in object-oriented programming
- [ ] Download the Java 2 Platform, Standard Edition
- [ ] Recognize the structure of a Java program
- [ ] Use the Java development cycle, which includes creating a source code file, compiling the source code, and executing a Java program

It is recommended that you do the exercises and labs in this chapter only after you have finished Chapter 4 of your book, *Programming Logic and Design*. In this chapter, you are introduced to the Java programming language and its history, learning about some introductory object-oriented concepts, compiling and executing a Java program, and learning how to download the Java 2 Platform, Standard Edition. You begin writing Java programs in Chapter 2 of this book.

THE JAVA PROGRAMMING LANGUAGE

The Java programming language was developed by Dr. James Gosling and introduced by Sun Microsystems in late 1995. Java has become very popular in a short period of time mostly due to the popularity of the World Wide Web. Java is an object-oriented programming language that can be used to create dynamic and interactive Web pages and to write Web-based applications that run on Web servers. **Web servers** are the computers that "serve up" content when you request to view Web pages. Examples of **Web-based applications** are an online bookstore and an online course registration system. Java is also used to develop **standalone enterprise applications**, which are programs that help manage data and run a business, and applications for cell phones and personal digital assistants.

Because Java is an object-oriented programming language, the programs you write using Java are object-oriented programs. When you write object-oriented programs, you use classes and objects and methods. You learn more about this object-oriented terminology later in this chapter.

The Java programming language is only a part of a system called the Java 2 platform. You will use the Java 2 platform when you write, compile, and execute Java programs in this book. The Java 2 platform includes many reusable libraries called packages. These **packages** are used by programmers to simplify their programming tasks when they reuse the predefined classes included in the libraries. Java is said to be powerful because the Java 2 platform also includes a group of development tools to be used by program developers. Examples of development tools include the **compiler** (javac), the **bytecode interpreter** (java), and the **appletviewer** (appletviewer).

TIP ▫ ▫ ▫ ▫ | Right now, you probably feel as though you are reading a book written in a foreign language. Many of the terms used to describe the Java 2 platform might be unfamiliar to you. You shouldn't worry about that right now. By the time you finish with this chapter, you will understand this new and exciting terminology. You also will be using some of the tools that are part of the Java 2 platform.

THREE TYPES OF JAVA PROGRAMS

Java programs can be written as applications, servlets, or applets. An **application** is a stand-alone program. A **servlet** is a Java program that runs on a Web server to provide the functionality allows the contents of Web pages to be viewed by people who use the World Wide Web. An **applet** is a Java program that is executed and viewed in a browser such as Netscape Navigator or Internet Explorer. With this book, you will write applications, which means you will be writing stand-alone Java programs.

AN INTRODUCTION TO OBJECT-ORIENTED TERMINOLOGY

Object-oriented programming is a programming method in which a program is made up of a collection of interacting objects. An **object** represents something in the real world, such as a car, an employee, or an item in an inventory. An object **encapsulates** data and behaviors, which means that the data and behaviors are contained within the object.

You refer to the data within an object as the object's attributes, and you refer to an object's behaviors as the object's methods. An **attribute** describes a characteristic of the object, such as its shape, its color, or its name. A **method** is a procedure or function, such as a method to calculate an employee's salary, that operates on the object's attributes. You communicate with objects in a program by passing messages. You pass **messages** by using an object to **invoke**, or call, one of its methods.

You will be doing object-oriented programming throughout this book because Java is an object-oriented language and insists that only object-oriented programs are written using the language. You must understand a few object-oriented concepts to be successful at reading and working with Java programs in your lab exercises. Note, however, that you will not learn enough to make you a Java programmer. You will have to take additional courses in Java to become a Java programmer. This book teaches you only the basics.

When Java programmers begin to write a program, they must begin by creating a class. A **class** can be thought of as a template for creating objects. In a class, the programmer specifies the data (attributes) and behaviors (methods) for all objects that belong to that class.

You can think of a class as a blueprint for the creation of objects. It specifies the attributes and methods that an object will have when created from a class. An object is sometimes referred to as an **instance** of a class, and the process of creating an object is referred to as **instantiation**.

A real-world example of "class," "instance," and "instantiation" coming together is a recipe for a chocolate cake and an actual chocolate cake. The recipe is similar to a class and the actual cake is an object. If you wanted to, you could create many chocolate cakes that are all based on the same recipe. In object-oriented programming, you can create as many objects as you need in your program from the same class.

DOWNLOADING THE JAVA 2 PLATFORM, STANDARD EDITION (J2SE) VERSION 1.4.2

All of the examples in this book have been written using the Java 2 Platform, Standard Edition (J2SE) version 1.4.2. You can get your own copy of the Java 2 Platform and install it on your computer at home, or your school may have the Java 2 Platform installed in your lab.

To get your own copy, go to the J2SE Web site at *http://java.sun.com/j2se/1.4.2/download.html*. Scroll down to the label Download J2SE v 1.4.2_0X. The "X" represents a digit that changes as Sun releases new downloads. Under the SDK column, click "download" then follow the directions for downloading and installing the software on your computer. Refer to the front of this book or ask your instructor if you have questions regarding this process.

THE STRUCTURE OF A JAVA PROGRAM

When a programmer learns a new programming language, traditionally the first program he or she writes is the Hello World program. This is done to illustrate that the language is capable of instructing the computer to communicate with the "outside" world. When this program executes, it simply displays the words "Hello World." on the user's screen. The Java version of the Hello World program is shown in Figure 1-1:

FIGURE 1-1: HELLO WORLD PROGRAM

```
public class HelloWorld
{
   public static void main(String args[])
   {
     System.out.println("Hello world.");
   }
}
```

TIP □ □ □ □ The programs you work with in this book are all written by first creating a class and including one method in that class. The class name will change but the name of the method will always be `main()` because it is always the first method that executes in a Java program.

As shown in Figure 1-1, you begin writing a class by using the keyword `public`, followed by the keyword `class`, followed by the name of the class. **Keywords** are special words that are reserved by Java to have a special meaning. You will learn more about Java's keywords in Chapter 2. The keyword `public` is needed to make the class available when you want to execute the program. The `class` keyword tells the Java compiler that you are beginning the creation of a class and that what follows is part of that class. The name of the class is up to you; however, the name should be meaningful. Because this program is written to display the words "Hello World." on the user's screen, I decided that the class would be named `HelloWorld`.

TIP □ □ □ □ In Java, it is a convention to begin class names with a capital letter. If a class name is made up of two or more words, the first letter of all words in the name is capitalized, but there is no space between the words.

On the next line is an opening curly brace (`{`). The opening curly brace marks the beginning of the Java code that is part of that class. Notice that there is a closing curly brace (`}`) on the last line of the code sample in Figure 1-1. This closing curly brace marks the end of the class named `HelloWorld`.

On the next line is the method named `main()`. This is a special method in a Java program; the `main()` method is the first method that executes when any program runs. The programs in this textbook will include only the `main()` method. When you learn more about Java, you will be able to include additional methods.

You begin writing the `main()` method by creating the header for the `main()` method. The **header** begins with the `public` keyword, followed by the `static` keyword, followed by the `void` keyword, followed by the method name, which is `main()`. The `public` keyword makes this method available for execution. The keyword `static` means you do not have to create a `HelloWorld` object to run the application.

TIP ▫ ▫ ▫ ▫ | A complete explanation for including the `static` keyword is beyond the scope of this book. For now, you have to include it to make your programs work. When you learn more about Java, you will understand why it must be included in this situation (yet not in all situations).

The `void` keyword indicates that the `main()` method does not return anything. Methods can be written to return a value, such as a number or a name. This is also something you will learn more about when you take a Java programming class.

The `main()` method is always written with `String args[]` within parentheses following the word `main`. This means that some arguments, or values, could be passed to the `main()` method. The full reason for doing this is also beyond the scope of this book, so, for now, you simply have to include it without understanding why. Remember that Java is a complex programming language; you will have to learn much more about it after you finish this course in order to become a Java programmer.

Following the header for `main()`, the next line begins with another opening curly brace. This curly brace marks the beginning of the code that is included in the `main()` method. Notice that on the second-to-last line of the code there is a closing curly brace. This curly brace marks the end of the `main()` method. All the code within this pair of curly braces executes when the `main()` method executes. For the examples in this book, this is all the code we want executed in our programs.

In Figure 1-1, there is only one line of code that executes when the `main()` method executes. This is the line that causes the words "Hello World." to appear on the user's screen. In Java, `System.out.println();` prints the string that is included within the parentheses following the word `println`. You can tell `println()` is a method because of the parentheses; all Java method names are followed by parentheses. A **string** is a series of characters and may be either a string constant or a `String` object. You learn more about `String` objects in the next chapter. In this example, a string constant is placed within the parentheses. A **string constant** is one or more characters that are placed within a pair of double quotation marks. Because we placed the characters "Hello World." within the double quotation marks, that is the string that appears.

TIP ▫ ▫ ▫ ▫ | In the statement `System.out.println("Hello World.");`, `System` is a class, `out` is an object, and `println()` is a method. Java programs frequently use this class-dot-object-dot-method syntax.

Note that the semicolon that ends the `System.out.println("Hello World.");` statement is required because it tells the compiler that this is the end of the statement. Next, you learn about the Java development cycle so that later in this chapter you can compile the Hello World program and execute it.

THE JAVA DEVELOPMENT CYCLE

When you finish designing a program and writing the Java code that implements your design, you will then want to compile and execute your program. This three-step process of writing code, compiling code, and executing code is called the Java Development Cycle. It is illustrated in Figure 1-2.

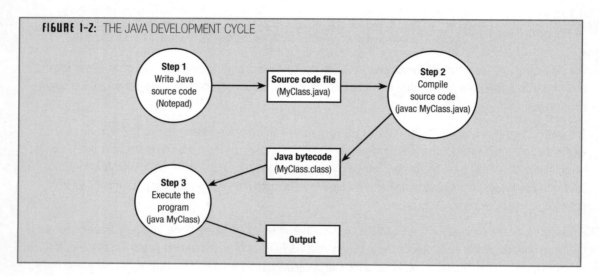

FIGURE 1-2: THE JAVA DEVELOPMENT CYCLE

Let's begin by learning about Step 1, writing the Java source code.

WRITING JAVA SOURCE CODE

As you learned in the previous section, you write a Java program by creating a class and including a method named `main()` in the class. But what do you use to write the program, and where do you save it?

To write a Java program, you use a text editor, such as the Windows text editor, which is Notepad. You can use any text editor, but in this book Notepad is assumed to be your text editor. You first must open Notepad by clicking Start, then Programs or All Programs, then Accessories, and then Notepad. When Notepad is started, you simply type your Java source code. **Source code** is the name used for the statements that make up a Java program.

Using Figure 1-1 from the previous section as an example, the source code includes the class `HelloWorld` and the `main()` method that is part of the class. After you have typed your source code, you then save the source code in a file that is referred to as your source code file. When you save the source code file, it is important to name the file using the same name as the class, and then add a .java extension. For the Hello World program, the class is named `HelloWorld`; therefore, the name of the source code file must be `HelloWorld.java`. Of course, it is also important to remember the location of the directory in which you choose to save your source code file.

TIP ▫ ▫ ▫ ▫   Notice that the name of the file and the name of the class must match exactly. This includes the use of uppercase and lowercase letters. It would not be correct to name the source code file `helloworld.java` because the lowercase *h* and lowercase *w* do not match the uppercase *H* and uppercase *W* used in the name of the class.

You move on to Step 2 after your source code file has been saved. Step 2 is to compile the source code.

COMPILING A JAVA PROGRAM

As you learned earlier in this chapter, the Java 2 platform contains several utility programs. One of these utilities is the Java compiler named javac. The javac compiler is responsible for taking your source code and transforming it into bytecode. **Bytecode** is intermediate, machine independent code. **Intermediate** means that the code is between source code and machine code. **Machine code** is the 1s and 0s that a computer needs to execute a program. The Java compiler automatically saves the intermediate bytecode in a file. This file has the same name as the source code file, but it has a .class extension rather than a .java extension. The bytecode generated by the compiler is platform independent. This is an important feature of Java. **Platform independence** means that the same Java program can be executed on many different types of computers that run many different operating systems.

The source code file `HelloWorld.java` is used in the example that follows. To compile your program, you follow these steps:

1. Set your PATH environment variable.

 **TIP** ▫ ▫ ▫ ▫ | The PATH environment variable tells your operating system which directories on your system contain commands.

2. Set your CLASSPATH environment variable.

TIP ▫ ▫ ▫ ▫ | The CLASSPATH environment variable tells your operating system which directories on your system contain resources it needs to run your program.

TIP ▫ ▫ ▫ ▫ | If you are working in a school computer lab, these steps might already have been accomplished for you. If you do not know how to set the PATH and CLASSPATH, see the front of this book or your instructor for further information.

3. Open a DOS window, and then at the DOS prompt, change to the directory that contains your source code file by using the DOS `cd` command.
4. At the DOS prompt, type the following command that uses the Java compiler—javac—to compile the program:

    ```
    javac HelloWorld.java
    ```

    If there are no syntax errors, a file named `HelloWorld.class` is created. You do not see anything special happen; you just return to the DOS prompt. This file contains the bytecode for the Hello World program. If there are syntax errors, you must go back to Notepad to fix the errors, save the source code file again, and recompile until there are no syntax errors remaining. **Syntax errors** are messages from the compiler that tell you what your errors are and where they are located in your source code file.

5. After the program is compiled, you can use the DOS `dir` command to do a directory listing to see the file named `HelloWorld.class`. It should be in the same directory as the source code file `HelloWorld.java`.

TIP ▫ ▫ ▫ ▫ | If you open a .class file using a text editor such as Notepad, what you see will be meaningless to you.

EXECUTING A JAVA PROGRAM

As you know, a computer can understand only machine code (1s and 0s), so a program must eventually be transformed into machine code before it can be executed. The **Java Virtual Machine (JVM)** is an **interpreter** that is responsible for transforming bytecode into machine code and then executing that machine code.

There are many JVMs available from different vendors and written for different purposes. For example, Web browsers, such as Internet Explorer and Netscape, contain a JVM. There is another JVM for the Windows operating system, another for the Mac operating system, and yet another for the Unix operating system. You will most likely use the Windows JVM when you execute your Java programs. The name of the Java 2 Platform utility you use to transform bytecode and execute your Java programs is java.

Step 3 in the development cycle is to execute the Java program. To execute the Hello World program, do the following:

1. Enter the following command at the DOS prompt:

```
java HelloWorld
```

TIP ▫ ▫ ▫ ▫ | You must be in the same directory that contains your .class file when you execute the program.

2. When the program executes, the words "Hello World." appear in a DOS window.

EXERCISE 1-1: UNDERSTANDING JAVA UTILITIES

In this exercise, you use what you have learned about using Java utilities to answer the following questions.

You have written a Java program and have stored your source code in a file named `MyFirstProgram.java`.

1. What is the name of the class stored in this file?

_____

2. What command would you use to compile the source code?

_____

3. What command would you use to execute the program?

_____

LAB 1-1: COMPILING AND EXECUTING A JAVA PROGRAM

In this lab, you compile and execute a prewritten Java program, and then answer some questions about the program.

1. Open the source code file named `Welcome.java` using Notepad or the text editor of your choice.

2. Save this source code file in a directory of your choice, and then change to that directory.

3. Compile the source code file. There should be no syntax errors. Record the command you used to compile the source code file.

   _____

4. Execute the program. Record the command you used to execute the program and also record the output of this program.

   _____

5. Modify the class so that it displays "Happy Birthday to you." Change the class name to `BirthdayGreeting`. Save the file as `BirthdayGreeting.java`. Compile the class and execute.

6. Modify the `BirthdayGreeting` class so that it prints two lines of output. Change the class name to `BirthdayGreeting2`. Add a second output statement that displays "Have a great day." Save the modified file as `BirthdayGreeting2.java`. Compile and execute.

2

VARIABLES, OPERATORS, AND WRITING PROGRAMS USING SEQUENTIAL STATEMENTS

After studying Chapter 2, you will be able to:

- ☐ Name variables and use appropriate data types
- ☐ Declare and initialize variables
- ☐ Use arithmetic operators in expressions and assignment operators in assignment statements
- ☐ Write Java comments
- ☐ Write programs using sequential statements

In this chapter, you are introduced to elements of the Java programming language that allow you to write programs that use sequential statements. We begin by reviewing variables and how you use them in a Java program. It is recommended that you do the exercises and labs in this chapter only after you have finished Chapter 4 of your book, *Programming Logic and Design*.

VARIABLES

You use a variable in a program when you need to store values. In Java, you must declare variables before you can use them in a program. Before you learn how to declare variables, you need to understand the rules you must follow when you give your variables a name. These rules are discussed in the following section.

VARIABLE NAMES

Variable names in Java can consist of letters, numerical digits, a dollar sign, and the underscore character, but they cannot begin with a digit. For example, `my_var`, `num6`, `intValue`, and `firstName` are all legal variable names in Java. Examples of invalid names are `3wrong`, `$don't`, and `public`. Because it begins with a digit `3wrong` is invalid; `$don't` is invalid because it contains a single quote; and `public` is invalid because it is a Java keyword. You cannot use a Java keyword for a variable name. A **keyword** is a word that the compiler reserves because it has a special meaning. You learn how to use some of Java's keywords later in this chapter and throughout this book.

When you name your variables, you must remember that Java is **case sensitive**. Java knows the difference between uppercase and lowercase characters. So the variables named `value`, `Value`, and `VaLuE` are three different variable names in Java.

The length of variable names is unlimited in Java. You can use as many characters as you want to name a variable. When you name variables, give them meaningful names that are long enough to describe how the variable is used, but not so long that you make your program hard to read or cause yourself unnecessary typing. For example, a variable named `firstName` clearly will be used in your program to store someone's first name. The variable named `freshmanStudentFirstName` is descriptive but long; a variable named `fn` is too short and not meaningful.

 It is a Java convention to begin the names of variables with a lowercase letter and to begin all other words in the name with an uppercase letter—for example, `firstName`. You do not include spaces between the words in a variable name.

JAVA DATA TYPES

Another rule for using variables in a Java program is that when you want to use a variable, you must specify a particular data type for that variable. A variable's **data type** dictates the amount of memory that is allocated and the range of values that you can store as a value in the variable. A **primitive** data type is one that is built into the language. There are eight primitive data types in Java: `byte`, `short`, `int`, `long`, `float`, `double`, `char`, and `boolean`.

You will not use all of these primitive data types in the programs you write in this book. The data types you will use are integers (`int`) or floating point values (`double`). You will use the `int` data type for values that are whole numbers. If you want to store someone's age (for example, 25) or the number of students in a class (for example, 35), you will specify the variables to hold those values as data type `int`. When you want to store a floating point value, such as the price of an item ($2.95) or a measurement (2.5 feet), you will use data type `double`. You will learn about using the other primitive data types as you continue to learn more about Java in subsequent courses.

You will also use strings in the programs you write in this book. A **string** is a group of one or more characters. An example of a string is the last name "Wallace" or a product type, such as a "desk". There is no primitive data type in Java for a string. None exists because, in Java, a string is an object, not a data type. An object is an instance of a class. When you use string variables in your programs, you are instantiating Java's `String` class, thereby creating the `String` objects you need for your program.

TIP □ □ □ □ | Even though `String` is a class and not a primitive data type, we will frequently refer to `String` as a data type for convenience.

EXERCISE 2-1: USING JAVA VARIABLES, DATA TYPES, AND KEYWORDS

In this exercise, you use what you have learned about naming Java variables, Java data types, and keywords to answer the following questions.

1. Is each of the following a legal Java variable name? (Answer yes or no.)

   my_var _____   i_am_a_variable _____   VALUE _____

   your_var _____   value _____ $value _____

   final* _____   num6 _____   intValue _____

   5May _____   numberOne _____   Value _____

   *note that this is a Java keyword

2. What data type (`int`, `double`, or `String`) is appropriate to store each of the following values?

   A person's age _____

   The amount of a discount, such as 15% _____

   The price of a birthday gift _____

   The name of a real estate agent _____

   The number of people you are inviting to your graduation party _____

DECLARING AND INITIALIZING VARIABLES

You must declare all Java variables before you can use them in your program. **Declaring** a variable tells the compiler that you are going to use the variable, and tells the compiler the variable's name and data type. This allows the compiler to reserve a memory location for the variable.

The Java syntax for declaring a variable is as follows:

data type variableName;

As an example of declaring a variable, the Java code `int counter;` declares a variable named `counter` with an `int` data type. The compiler reserves 32 bits (4 bytes) of memory for the variable named `counter`, and the name `counter` now is associated with the memory address 1000, as shown in Figure 2-1.

FIGURE 2-1: DECLARATION OF VARIABLE AND MEMORY ALLOCATION

```
int counter;
```

counter (variable name)				another variable	
value of counter				value of the next variable	
first byte	second byte	third byte	fourth byte		

1000 (The memory address is assigned by the compiler; you cannot assign the memory address yourself.)

1004 (This is the next available memory address after `counter` because 4 bytes [1000, 1001, 1002, and 1003] have been reserved for the variable named `counter`.)

You can also initialize a Java variable when you declare it. When you **initialize** a Java variable, you give it an initial value at the same time you declare it. For example, you can assign an initial value of 8 to the `counter` variable when you declare it, as shown in the following code:

```
int counter = 8;
```

TIP □ □ □ □   Variables are automatically initialized to zero (0) if you do not specify a different value.

You can also declare and initialize variables of data type `double` and variables of data type `String`, as shown in the following code:

```
double salary;
double cost = 12.95;
String firstName;
String homeAddress = "123 Main Street";
```

You can declare more than one variable in one statement as long as they have the same data type, like so:

```
int counter, value;
```

EXERCISE 2-2: DECLARING AND INITIALIZING JAVA VARIABLES

In this exercise, you use what you have learned about declaring and initializing Java variables.

1. Write a Java variable declaration for each of the following. Use data type `int`, `double`, or `String`, and choose meaningful variable names.

   Declare a variable to store a student's numeric test score (0–100). _____

Declare a variable to store the number of students in a class. _____

Declare a variable to store the price of an item. _____

Declare a variable to store the name of your favorite TV program. _____

2. Declare and initialize variables to represent the following values. Use data type `int`, `double`, or `String`, and choose meaningful variable names.

The side of a rectangle is 6.5 inches in length. _____

The number of vacation days you have not used this year is 12. _____

The answer to a question is "Yes". _____

The number of pets you have is 2. _____

LAB 2-1: DECLARING AND INITIALIZING JAVA VARIABLES

In this lab, you declare and initialize variables in a prewritten Java program. The program is written to calculate your age in the year 2010.

1. Open the source code file named `MyAge.java` using Notepad or the text editor of your choice.

2. Declare an integer variable named `myCalculatedAge`.

3. Declare and initialize an integer variable named `myCurrentAge`. Initialize this variable with your current age.

4. Declare and initialize an integer variable named `thisYear`. Initialize this variable with the value of the current year. Use four digits for the year.

5. Save this source code file in a directory of your choice, and then make that directory your working directory.

6. Compile the source code file `MyAge.java`.

7. Execute the program. Record the output of this program.

_____

_____

ARITHMETIC AND ASSIGNMENT OPERATORS

An **operator** is a symbol that tells the computer to perform a mathematical or logical operation. Java has a large assortment of operators. We begin the discussion with a group of operators known as the arithmetic operators.

ARITHMETIC OPERATORS

You use the arithmetic operators to perform arithmetic calculations as part of your programs. Table 2-1 lists Java's arithmetic operator names and symbols, examples of their use, and comments that further explain their use.

TABLE 2-1: JAVA ARITHMETIC OPERATORS

Operator Name and Symbol	Example	Comment
Addition +	num1 + num2	
Subtraction −	num1 − num2	
Multiplication *	num1 * num2	
Division /	15/2	Integer division; result is 7; fraction is truncated.
	15.0 / 2.0	Floating point division; result is 7.5.
	15.0 / 2	Floating point division; result is 7.5.
Modulus %	hours % 24	Performs division and finds the remainder; result is 1 if the value of hours is 25.
Unary plus +	+num1	Maintains the value of the expression; if the value of num1 is 3, then +num1 is 3.
Unary minus −	-(num1 − num2)	If value of (num1 − num2) is 10, then -(num1 − num2) is −10.

You can combine arithmetic operators and variables to create **expressions**. The computer evaluates each expression, and the result is a value. To give you an idea of how this works, assume that the value of num1 is 3 and num2 is 20, and both are data type int. With this information, note the following examples of expressions and their values:

- num1 + num2 evaluates to 23
- num1 − num2 evaluates to −17
- num2 % num1 evaluates to 2
- num1 * num2 evaluates to 60
- num2 / num1 evaluates to 6
- -num1 evaluates to -3

ASSIGNMENT OPERATORS AND THE ASSIGNMENT STATEMENT

When you want to store values in variables, you use Java's assignment operators to write assignment statements. Table 2-2 lists some of Java's assignment operators along with their symbols, an example, and comments that further explain their use.

TABLE 2-2: JAVA ASSIGNMENT OPERATORS

Operator Name and Symbol	Example	Comment
Assignment =	`count = 5;`	Places the value on the right side into the memory location named on the left side.
Initialization =	`int count = 5;`	Places the value on the right side into the memory location named on the left side when the variable is declared.
Assignment +=	`num += 20;`	Equivalent to `num = num + 20;`
-=	`num -= 20;`	Equivalent to `num = num - 20;`
*=	`num *= 20;`	Equivalent to `num = num * 20;`
/=	`num /= 20;`	Equivalent to `num = num / 20;`
%=	`num %= 20;`	Equivalent to `num = num % 20;`

When an assignment statement executes, the computer evaluates the expression on the right side of the assignment operator and then assigns the result to the memory location associated with the variable named on the left side of the assignment operator. An example of an assignment statement is shown in the following code. Notice that the statement ends with a semicolon. In Java, assignment statements always end with a semicolon.

```
answer = num1 * num2;
```

This assignment statement causes the computer to evaluate the expression `num1 * num2`. Then the computer stores the results in the memory location associated with `answer`. If the value stored in the variable named `num1` is 3, and the value stored in the variable named `num2` is 20, then the value 60 is assigned to the variable named `answer`.

Here is another example:

```
answer += num1;
```

This statement is equivalent to the following statement:

```
answer = answer + num1;
```

If the value of `answer` is currently 10, and the value of `num1` is 3, then the expression on the right side of the assignment statement `answer + num1;` evaluates to 13, and the computer assigns the value 13 to `answer`.

PRECEDENCE AND ASSOCIATIVITY

Precedence refers to the order in which the compiler performs operations. Operators have different precedence associated with them. Operators also have **associativity**, which refers to the order in which operations are evaluated when operators have the same precedence. Table 2-3 shows the precedence and associativity of the operators discussed in this chapter.

TABLE 2-3: ORDER OF PRECEDENCE AND ASSOCIATIVITY

Operator Name	Operator Symbol(s)	Order of Precedence	Associativity
Parentheses	( )	First	Left to right
Unary	– +	Second	Right to left
Multiplication, division, and modulus	* / %	Third	Left to right
Addition and subtraction	+ –	Fourth	Left to right
Assignment	= += –+ *= /= %=	Fifth	Right to left

The parentheses operator, `( )`, has the highest precedence. You use this operator to change the order in which operations are performed. For example, look at the following:

```
average = test1 + test2 / 2;
```

In this example, you want to find the average of two test scores. If the value of `test1` is 90 and the value of `test2` is 88, then the value assigned to `average` will be 134! This is not what you intended, but it is what the code will provide because the precedence of operations causes the division, `test2 / 2`, to occur before the addition operation. You must use the parentheses operator in this example to force the addition to occur before the division. The correct statement looks like this:

```
average = (test1 + test2) / 2;
```

In this example, the value of `test1`, 90, is added to the value of `test2`, 88, and then the sum is divided by 2. The value assigned to `average` is 89 and is the correct result.

EXERCISE 2-3: UNDERSTANDING OPERATOR PRECEDENCE AND ASSOCIATIVITY

Study the code that follows, and then answer the subsequent questions.

```
// This program demonstrates the precedence and
// associativity of operators.
public class Operators
{
```

```
public static void main(String args[])
{
    int num1 = 5;
    int num2 = 2;
    int num3 = 7;
    int result1, result2, result3;
    int result4, result5, result6;

    result1 = num1 * num2 + num3;
    System.out.println("Result 1: " + result1);

    result2 = num1 * (num2 + num3);
    System.out.println("Result 2: " + result2);

    result3 = num1 + num2 - num3;
    System.out.println("Result 3: " + result3);

    result4 = num1 + (num2 - num3);
    System.out.println("Result 4: " + result4);

    result5 = num1 + num2 * num3;
    System.out.println("Result 5: " + result5);

    result6 = num3 / num2;
    System.out.println("Result 6: " + result6);
    System.exit(0);
}
}
```

1. What is the value of `result1`? `result2`? `result3`? `result4`? `result5`? and
`result6`? Explain how precedence and associativity affect the result.

_____

_____

_____

_____

_____

_____

LAB 2-2: WORKING WITH ARITHMETIC AND ASSIGNMENT OPERATORS

In this lab, you complete a prewritten Java program that is written for a furniture company. The program prints the name of a furniture item, its retail price, its wholesale price, the profit made on the furniture item, a sale price, and the profit made when the sale price is used.

1. Open the file named `Furniture.java` using Notepad or the text editor of your choice.
2. Variables have been declared for you and the input statements and output statements have been written. Read them carefully before you proceed to the next step.
3. Design the logic that will use assignment statements to first calculate the profit, then calculate the sale price, and finally calculate the profit when the sale price is used. Profit is defined as the retail price minus the wholesale price. The sale price is 10% deducted from the retail price. The sale profit is defined as the sale price minus the wholesale price. Perform the appropriate calculations as part of your assignment statements.
4. Save the source code file in a directory of your choice, and then make that directory your working directory.
5. Compile the program.
6. Execute the program. Your output should be as follows:

   Item Name: Sofa

   Retail Price: $450.0

   Wholesale Price: $300.0

   Profit: $150.0

   Sale Price: $405.0

   Sale Profit: $105.0

JAVA COMMENTS

You use comments in your Java programs to describe or explain your logic to people who read your source code. The Java compiler ignores comments.

You will use two commenting styles when you write Java programs. For the first style, you type the `//` characters at the beginning of each comment line. For the second style, you enclose a block of text with the characters `/*` and `*/`. The `//` comment style is used for single line comments. The block comment markers are useful when your comment spans several lines. You may place comments anywhere in a Java program. The following code sample illustrates both styles of comments:

```
/* These lines are a multi-line, block comment.
   This program prints Hello World on the user's screen.
*/
/*
```

```
This is a multi-line comment. The HelloWorld class has a
single method named main().
*/
public class HelloWorld
{
   // Class methods (Single line comment).
   public static void main(String args[])
   {
      System.out.println("Hello World");
   } // End of main method (Single line comment).
} // End of HelloWorld class (Single line comment).
```

TIP □ □ □ □ | You are responsible for including well-written, meaningful comments in all the programs you write. In fact, some programmers think that commenting your source code is as important as the source code itself.

SEQUENTIAL STATEMENTS

You use a sequence in programs when you want to perform actions one after the other. A sequence can contain any number of actions, but those actions must be in the proper order, and actions contained within the sequence cannot be skipped. The Java program in the following example uses sequential statements to convert a Fahrenheit temperature to its Celsius equivalent:

```
/* This Java program converts a Fahrenheit temperature to Celsius.
Input: Interactive.
Output: Fahrenheit temperature followed by Celsius temperature.
*/
import javax.swing.JOptionPane; // Import JOptionPane class.
public class Temperature
{
   public static void main(String args[])
   {
      String fahrenheitString;
      double fahrenheit;
      double celsius;

      // Get user input.
      fahrenheitString = JOptionPane.showInputDialog(
         "Enter Fahrenheit temperature: ");
      // Convert String to double.
      fahrenheit = Double.parseDouble(fahrenheitString);
      // Calculate Celsius equivalent.
```

```
            celsius = (fahrenheit - 32.0) * (5.0/9.0);
            // Output.
            System.out.println("Fahrenheit temperature:" +
                                fahrenheit);
            System.out.println("Celsius temperature:" + celsius);
            // End program.
            System.exit(0);
        }
    }
```

This program is made up of sequential statements that execute one after the other. After the variables `fahrenheitString`, `fahrenheit`, and `celsius` are declared, the first statement that executes is the assignment statement, as follows:

```
        fahrenheitString = JOptionPane.showInputDialog(
            "Enter Fahrenheit temperature:");
```

The `showInputDialog` method used on the right side of the assignment statement belongs to the `JOptionPane` class and is used when you want a program user to interactively input data needed by your program. This method may be used in this program because the `JOptionPane` class was imported into this program using the following statement: `import javax.swing.JOptionPane;`. When you **import** a class, a program then has access to the methods that are part of that class. When you use the `showInputDialog` method, you specify within parentheses the words you want to appear in the dialog box on the user's screen. In this example, the phrase "Enter Fahrenheit temperature:" will appear. The dialog box also displays a text area where the user types his or her input, as shown in Figure 2-2.

FIGURE 2-2: AN INPUT DIALOG BOX

In this program, you want the user to input a Fahrenheit temperature value so the program can convert it to Celsius. The Fahrenheit value input by the user is assigned to the `String` variable named `fahrenheitString`, as this is the variable named on the left side of the assignment statement. Whatever the user inputs in the text area of an input dialog box is always considered a `String`; therefore it must be assigned to a `String` variable.

The second statement to execute is also an assignment statement, as follows:

```
        fahrenheit = Double.parseDouble(fahrenheitString);
```

The `parseDouble` method is used on the right side of this assignment statement. This method belongs to the `Double` class and is used to convert the `String` representation of the Fahrenheit value to data type `double`.

Once the `string` is converted to `double`, it is assigned to the variable `fahrenheit`, which is declared as a `double`. You must convert the `string` to a `double` to perform the arithmetic operations needed to convert a Fahrenheit temperature to its Celsius equivalent.

The third statement to execute is another assignment statement, as follows:

```
celsius = (fahrenheit - 32.0) * (5.0/9.0);
```

The formula to convert Fahrenheit temperatures to Celsius is used on the right side of this assignment statement. Notice the use of parentheses in the expression to control precedence. The expression is evaluated and the resulting value is assigned to the variable named `celsius`.

TIP □ □ □ □ | Notice that the division uses the values 5.0 and 9.0. This is floating-point division, which results in a value that includes a fraction. If the values 5 and 9 were used, integer division would be performed, and the fractional portion would be truncated.

The next two statements to execute in sequence are both output statements, as follows:

```
System.out.println("Fahrenheit temperature:" +
                            fahrenheit);
System.out.println("Celsius temperature:" + celsius);
```

The statement `System.out.println` is used to output whatever is within the parentheses. The first output statement displays the words "Fahrenheit temperature:", followed by the value stored in the variable `fahrenheit`. The second output statement displays the words "Celsius temperature: ", followed by the value stored in the variable `celsius`. The + symbol, when used in this context, is the **concatenation** operator, not the addition operator. It is used to combine two values next to each other to create a single string.

The last statement in this program is `System.exit(0);`. This statement is used to end or terminate a Java program.

Now that you have seen a complete Java program that uses sequential statements, it is time for you to begin writing your own programs.

EXERCISE 2-4: UNDERSTANDING SEQUENTIAL STATEMENTS

In this exercise, you use what you have learned about sequential statements to read a scenario, and then you answer the subsequent questions.

You have written a Java program to calculate how much wallpaper you must purchase to cover the walls in your study. Two of the walls are 8 feet high and 12.5 feet wide. The other two walls are 8 feet high and 15.2 feet wide. The salesperson at the home improvement store told you to buy 1 roll of wallpaper for every 50 square feet of wall you need to cover. The following code is what you have written, but your program is not compiling. Take a few minutes to study this code, and then answer Questions 1–4.

```
// Calculates the number of wallpaper rolls needed.
public class WallPaper
{
    public static void main(String args[])
    {
        double height1 = 8;
        double height2 = 8;
        int width1 = 12.5;
        double width2 = 15.2;
        double squareFeet;
        int numRolls;
        numRolls = squareFeet / 50;
        squareFeet = width1 * height1 + width2 * height2;
        System.out.println("Number of Rolls: " + numRolls);
        System.exit(0);
    }
}
```

1. The first error you receive from the javac compiler is as follows:

   ```
   WallPaper.java:8: possible loss of precision
   found    : double
   required: int
        int width1 = 12.5;
   ```

   What do you have to do to fix this problem? _____

2. The second error you receive from the javac compiler is this:

   ```
   WallPaper.java:12: possible loss of precision
   found    : double
   required: int
          numRolls = squareFeet / 50;
   ```

   What must you do to fix this problem? _____

3. Even if you fix the problems identified in Question 1 and Question 2, you will still have a problem with this program. It has to do with the order in which your statements are written. Identify the problem, and then determine what must be done. On the following lines, describe how to fix the problem.

   _____

   _____

   _____

4. You have two variables declared in this program to represent the height of your walls, `height1` and `height2`. Do you need both of these variables? If no, how would you change the program? Be sure to identify all of the changes you would make.

_____

_____

_____

_____

_____

LAB 2-3: USING SEQUENTIAL STATEMENTS IN A JAVA PROGRAM

In this lab, you complete a prewritten Java program. The program is written to calculate the withholding taken from an employee's weekly salary, the tax deduction to which the employee is entitled for each dependent, and the employee's take-home pay. The program output includes State Tax withheld, Federal Tax withheld, dependent tax deductions, salary, and take-home pay.

1. Open the source code file named `Salary.java` using Notepad or the text editor of your choice.
2. Variables have been declared and initialized for you, as needed, and the input and output statements have been written. Read the code carefully before you proceed to the next step.
3. Write the Java code needed to perform the following:
   - Calculate state withholding tax at 7.5% and calculate federal withholding tax at 28.0%.
   - Calculate dependent deductions at 5.0% of the employee's salary for each dependent.
   - Calculate total withholding.
   - Calculate take-home pay as salary minus total withholding plus deductions.
4. Save this source code file in a directory of your choice, and then make that directory your working directory.
5. Compile the program.
6. Execute the program. You should get the following output:

   State Tax: $56.25

   Federal Tax: $210.00000000000003

   Dependents: $75.0

   Salary: $750.0

   Take-Home Pay: $558.75

TIP ▫ ▫ ▫ ▫ | You cannot control the number of places after the decimal point when you want to output floating point values until you learn more about Java.

3

WRITING PROGRAMS THAT MAKE DECISIONS

After studying Chapter 3, you will be able to:

☐ Use relational and logical Boolean operators to make decisions in a program

☐ Compare `String` objects

☐ Write decision statements in Java, including an `if` statement, an `if else` statement, and nested `if` statements

☐ Use decision statements to make multiple comparisons by using AND logic and OR logic

It is recommended that you do the exercises and labs in this chapter only after you have finished Chapter 5 of your book, *Programming Logic and Design*. In this chapter, you practice using Java's relational and logical operators as well as `String` methods to write Boolean expressions. You also learn the Java syntax for decision statements, including the `if` statement, the `if-else` statement, and nested `if` statements. Finally, you learn to write Java statements that make multiple comparisons.

BOOLEAN OPERATORS

You use Boolean operators in expressions when you want to compare two values or when you want to make multiple comparisons in an expression. When you use a Boolean operator in an expression, the evaluation of that expression results in a value that is `true` or `false`. In Java, you can subdivide the **Boolean operators** into two groups: relational operators and logical operators. We begin the discussion with the relational operators.

RELATIONAL OPERATORS

In the context of programming, the term **relational** refers to the connections that values can have with one another. You can also think of this as how one value relates to another. As an example of this relationship or connection, you can compare one value to another in an expression to see if it is greater than, less than, or equal to the other value. In other words, the use of relational operators allows you to ask a question that results in a `true` or `false` answer. Depending on the answer, your program will execute different statements that perform different actions.

Table 3-1 lists the relational operators used in Java.

TABLE 3-1: RELATIONAL OPERATORS

Operator	Meaning
<	Less than
<=	Less than or equal to
>	Greater than
>=	Greater than or equal to
==	Equal to (two equal signs with no space between them)
!=	Not equal to

To see how to use the relational operators, suppose you declare two variables, an `int` named `number1` that you initialize with the value `10` and another `int` variable named `number2` that you initialize with the value `15`, as shown in the following code:

```
int number1 = 10;
int number2 = 15;
```

If you use the preceding code as the basis for our discussion, then the following code samples illustrate how the relational operators are used in expressions:

- `number1 < number2` evaluates to `true` because `10` is less than `15`.
- `number1 <= number2` evaluates to `true` because `10` is less than or equal to `15`.
- `number1 > number2` evaluates to `false` because `10` is not greater than `15`.
- `number1 >= number2` evaluates to `false` because `10` is not greater than or equal to `15`.
- `number1 == number2` evaluates to `false` because `10` is not equal to `15`.
- `number1 != number2` evaluates to `true` because `10` is not equal to `15`.

LOGICAL OPERATORS

You use logical operators when you need to ask more than one question but get only one answer. For example, in a program, you may want to ask if a number is between the values 1 and 10. To get an answer to this question, you can ask if the number is greater than or equal to 1 AND if the number is less than or equal to 10. You are asking two questions but you want only one answer, either yes (true) or no (false).

TIP ▫ ▫ ▫ ▫ | Logical operators are also Boolean operators. The term **logical** refers to the ways in which true and false values can be connected.

Referring to the example in the previous paragraph, you asked two questions that both result in a true or false answer, but the two answers are now combined, or connected, to give you a single true or false answer. They are useful in decision statements because, like relational expressions, they evaluate to `true` or `false`, thereby permitting decision-making in your programs.

Table 3-2 lists the logical operators used in Java.

TABLE 3-2: LOGICAL OPERATORS

Operator	Name	Description
`&&`	AND	All expressions must evaluate to `true` for the entire expression to be `true`; this operator is written as two `&` symbols with no space between them.
`||`	OR	Only one expression must evaluate to `true` for the entire expression to be `true`; this operator is written as two `|` symbols with no space between them.
`!`	NOT	This operator reverses the value of the expression; if the expression evaluates to `false`, then reverse it so that the expression evaluates to `true`.

To see how to use the logical operators, suppose you declare two variables: an `int` named `number1` that you initialize with the value `10`; and another `int` variable named `number2` that you initialize with the value `15`, as shown in the following code:

```
int number1 = 10;
int number2 = 15;
```

If you use the preceding code as the basis for our discussion, then the following code samples illustrate how you can use the logical operators along with the relational operators in expressions:

- `(number1 > number2) || (number1 == 10)` evaluates to `true` because the first expression evaluates to `false`, `10` is not greater than `15`, and the second expression evaluates to `true`, `10` is equal to `10`. Only one expression needs to be `true` using OR logic for the entire expression to be `true`.

- `(number1 > number2) && (number1 == 10)` evaluates to `false` because the first expression is `false`, `10` is not greater than `15`, and the second expression is `true`, `10` is equal to `10`. Using AND logic both expressions must be `true` for the entire expression to be `true`.

- `(number1 != number2) && (number1 == 10)` evaluates to `true` because both expressions are `true`; that is, `10` is not equal to `15` and `10` is equal to `10`. Using AND logic, if both expressions are `true`, then the entire expression is `true`.

- `!(number1 == number2)` evaluates to `true` because the expression evaluates to `false`, `10` is not equal to `15`, and reversing the value `false` results in a `true` value.

COMPARING STRINGS

In Java, you use relational operators when you compare primitive data types such as `ints` and `doubles`. As you have learned, a primitive data type is one that is built in to the language. You do not use the relational operators when you want to compare `Strings` in Java. In fact, it should not be done because you would be comparing references to the `String` objects, not the contents of the `String` objects. A **reference** is the location in memory where an object is stored. This is discussed further in Chapter 6 of this book.

When you declare a `String` variable, the declaration instantiates the `String` class and creates a `String` object. The `String` class contains multiple methods you can use when you want to compare `String` objects. One of these methods is the `equals()` method. You use it when you want to test two `String` objects for equality. The `equals()` method returns `true` if the two `String` objects are equal, and `false` if they are not.

TIP □ □ □ □ | Two `String` objects are equal when their contents are the same.

The following code shows how to use the `equals()` method with two `String` objects, with a single `String` object, and with a string constant.

```
String s1 = "Hello";
String s2 = "World";
// Evaluates to false because "Hello" is not the same as
// "World".
s1.equals(s2);
// Evaluates to true because "Hello" is the same as
// "Hello".
s1.equals("Hello");
```

In Java, it is important not to use the == operator to compare `String` objects. As you learned earlier in this chapter, using a relational operator is not an error, but it will test to see if two `String` objects are the same object (have identical references) instead of whether they have the same contents. The only time one `String` object would have the same reference value as another is when they are the same object. This would be like testing to see if `String1` is equal to `String1`. This is a trivial comparison because it will always be true and thus should not be undertaken.

Another method used to compare `String` objects is the `compareTo()` method. It returns a 0 if two `String` objects are equal, a value less than 0 if the invoking `String` object is less than the `String` object passed to the method, and a value greater than 0 if the invoking `String` object is greater than the `String` object passed to the method.

As shown in Figure 3-1, `s1` is the invoking `String` object, and `s2` is the `String` object passed to the method.

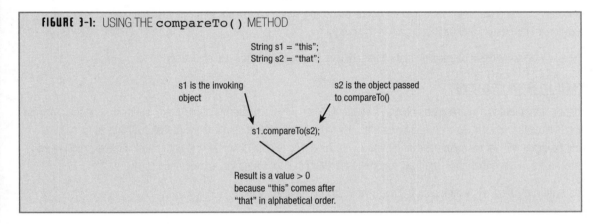

FIGURE 3-1: USING THE `compareTo()` METHOD

```
String s1 = "this";
String s2 = "that";
```

s1 is the invoking object

s2 is the object passed to compareTo()

s1.compareTo(s2);

Result is a value > 0 because "this" comes after "that" in alphabetical order.

The `compareTo()` method compares the ASCII values of the individual characters in `String` objects to determine if one `String` object is greater than, less than, or equal to another, in terms of alphabetizing the text in the `String` objects. As shown in Figure 3-1, the `String` object `s1`, whose value is "`this`", is greater than the `String` object `s2`, whose value is "`that`", because "`this`" comes after "`that`" in alphabetical order. The result of using the `compareTo()` method with `String` objects `s1` and `s2` is a value greater than 0 because "`this`" is greater than "`that`".

The following code sample shows how to use the `compareTo()` method with two `String` objects:

```
String s1 = "whole";
String s2 = "whale";
// The next statement evaluates to a value greater than
// 0 because the contents of s1, "whole", is greater
// than the contents of s2, "whale".
s1.compareTo(s2);
// The next statement evaluates to a value less than 0
// because the contents of s2, "whale", is less than the
// contents of s1, "whole".
s2.compareTo(s1);
```

The following code sample shows how to use the `compareTo()` method to compare a `String` object and a string constant:

```
String s1 = "whole";
s1.compareTo("whole");
```

DECISION STATEMENTS

Every decision in a program is based on whether an expression evaluates to `true` or `false`. Programmers use decision statements to change the flow of control in a program. **Flow of control** means the order in which statements are executed. Decision statements are also known as branching statements because they cause the computer to make a decision and then take a branch or a path in the program.

There are different types of decision statements in Java. We begin with the `if` statement.

THE IF STATEMENT

The `if` statement is a single-path decision statement. When we use the term "single-path," we mean that if an expression evaluates to `true`, your program executes one or more statements, but if the expression evaluates to `false`, your program will not execute these statements. There is only one path defined—the path taken if the expression evaluates to `true`. In either case, the next statement following the `if` statement is executed.

The syntax, or rules, for writing an `if` statement in Java is as follows:

```
if(expression)
    statementA;
```

Note that when you use the keyword `if` to begin an `if` statement, you follow it with an expression placed within parentheses.

When an `if` statement is encountered in a program, the expression within the parentheses is evaluated. If the expression evaluates to `true`, then the computer executes *statementA*. If the expression in parentheses evaluates to `false`, then the computer will not execute *statementA*. Remember that regardless of whether the expression evaluates to `true` and executes *statementA*, or the expression evaluates to `false` and does not execute *statementA*, the statement following the `if` executes next.

A Java statement can be either a simple statement or a block statement. A **block** statement is made up of multiple Java statements. Java defines a block as statements placed within a pair of curly braces. If you want your program to execute more than one statement as part of an `if` statement, you must enclose the statements in a pair of curly braces or only one statement will execute. The following example illustrates an `if` statement that uses the relational operator < to test if the value of the variable `customerAge` is less than 65. You will see the first curly brace in the third line and the second curly brace in the second-to-last line.

```
int customerAge = 53;
if(customerAge < 65)
{
    discount = 0;
    numUnder_65 += 1;
}
System.out.println("Discount : " + discount);
```

In the preceding code, the variable named `customerAge` was initialized to the value 53. Because 53 is less than 65, the expression, `customerAge` < 65, evaluates to `true` and the block statement executes. The block statement is made up of the two assignment statements within the curly braces: `discount = 0;` and `numUnder_65 += 1;`. If the expression evaluates to `false`, the block statement does not execute. In either case, the next statement to execute is the output statement, `System.out.println("Discount : " + discount);`.

Notice that you do not include a semicolon at the end of the line with the `if` and the expression to be tested. Doing so is not a syntax error, but it can create a logic error in your program. A **logic error** causes your program to produce incorrect results. In Java, the semicolon (`;`) is called the null statement and is considered a legal statement. The **null** statement is a statement that does nothing. Examine the following code:

```
if(customerAge < 65); // Semicolon here is not correct.
{
    discount = 0;
    numUnder_65 += 1;
}
```

If you write an `if` statement as shown in the preceding code, your program will test the expression `customerAge` < 65. If it evaluates to `true`, the null statement executes, which means your program does nothing, and then the statement `discount = 0;` executes because this is the next statement following the `if` statement. This does not cause a logic error in your program, but consider what happens when the expression in the `if` statement evaluates to `false`. If `false`, the null statement does not execute, but the statement `discount = 0;` executes because it is the next statement after the `if` statement.

The following code uses an `if` statement along with the `equals()` method to test two `String` objects for equality:

```
String dentPlan = "Y";
if(dentPlan.equals("Y"))
    grossPay = grossPay - 23.50;
```

In this example, if the value of the `String` object named `dentPlan` and the string constant `"Y"` are the same value, the expression evaluates to `true`, and the `grossPay` calculation assignment statement executes. If the expression evaluates to `false`, the `grossPay` calculation assignment statement does not execute.

EXERCISE 3-1: UNDERSTANDING IF STATEMENTS

In this exercise, you use what you have learned about writing `if` statements in Java to study a complete Java program that uses `if` statements. Take a few minutes to study the code that follows, and then answer Questions 1–4.

```java
public class Exercise3_1
{
  public static void main(String args[])
  {
    int testScore;
    String testGrade = "Pass";
    testScore = 60;
    if(testScore < 60)
      testGrade = "Fail";
    System.out.println("Test score: " + testScore);
    System.out.println("Test grade: " + testGrade);
    System.exit(0);
  }
}
```

1. What is the exact output when this program executes?

   _____

   _____

2. What is the exact output if the value of **testScore** is changed to **59**?

   _____

   _____

3. What is the exact output if the expression in the `if` statement is changed to
   `testScore <= 60` ?

   _____

   _____

4. What is the exact output if the variable named **testGrade** is initialized with the value "**Fail**" rather than the value "**Pass**"?

   _____

   _____

LAB 3-1: USING IF STATEMENTS

In this lab, you complete a prewritten Java program for a carpenter. The program is supposed to compute the price of any desk a customer orders, based on the following facts:

- The charge for all desks is a minimum of $200.00.
- If the surface (length * width) is over 750 square inches, add $50.00.

- If the wood is "mahogany" add $150.00; for "oak," add $125.00. No charge is added for "pine."
- For every drawer in the desk, there is an additional $30.00 charge.

1. Open the file named **Lab3_1.java** using Notepad or the text editor of your choice.
2. You need to declare variables for the following, and initialize them where specified:
   - A variable for the cost of the desk initialized to 0.00.
   - A variable for the length of the desk initialized to 60 inches.
   - A variable for the width of the desk initialized to 48 inches.
   - A variable for the surface area of the desk.
   - A variable for the wood type initialized with the value "oak".
   - A variable for the number of drawers initialized with the value 3.
3. Write the rest of the program using assignment statements and **if** statements as appropriate. The output statements are written for you.
4. Compile the program.
5. Execute the program. Your output should be: The charge for this desk is $465.0. Note that you cannot control the number of places that appear after the decimal point until you learn more about Java.

THE IF ELSE STATEMENT

The **if else** statement is a dual-path decision statement. That is, your program will take one of two paths as a result of evaluating an expression in an **if else** statement.

The syntax, or rules, for writing an **if else** statement in Java is as follows:

```
if(expression)
    statementA;
else
    statementB;
```

TIP □ □ □ □ Do not include a semicolon at the end of the line with the **if** and the expression to be tested, or on the line with the keyword **else**. As you learned earlier, doing so is not a syntax error, but it can create a logic error in your program.

When an **if else** statement is encountered in a program, the expression in the parentheses is evaluated. If the expression evaluates to **true**, then the computer executes *statementA*. Otherwise, if the expression in parentheses evaluates to **false**, then the computer executes *statementB*. Both *statementA* and *statementB* can be simple statements or block statements. Regardless of which path is taken in a program, the statement following the **if else** statement is the next one to execute.

The following code sample illustrates an `if else` statement written in Java:

```
int hoursWorked = 45;
String overtime;
double grossPay;
double rate = 15.00;
if(hoursWorked > 40)
{
   overtime = "Yes";
   grossPay = 40 * rate + (hoursWorked - 40) *
             1.5 * rate;
}
else
{
   overtime = "No";
   grossPay = hoursWorked * rate;
}
System.out.println("Gross Pay: $" + grossPay);
```

In the preceding code, the value of the `hoursWorked` variable is tested to see if it is greater than `40`. You use the relational operator, `>`, to make the comparison. If the `hoursWorked > 40` expression evaluates to `true`, then the block statement executes. This first block statement contains one statement that assigns the string constant "`Yes`" to the variable named `overtime`, and another statement that calculates the employee's gross pay, including overtime pay, and assigns the calculated value to the variable named `grossPay`.

If the expression `hoursWorked > 40` evaluates to `false`, then a different path is followed, and the second block statement following the keyword `else` executes. This block statement contains one statement that assigns the string constant "`No`" to the variable named `overtime`, and another statement that calculates the employee's gross pay with no overtime, and assigns the calculated value to the variable named `grossPay`.

Regardless of which path is taken in this code, the next statement to execute is the output statement, `System.out.println("Gross Pay: $" + grossPay);`.

EXERCISE 3-2: UNDERSTANDING IF ELSE STATEMENTS

In this exercise, you use what you have learned about writing `if else` statements in Java to study a complete Java program that uses `if else` statements. This program was written to calculate customer charges for a telephone company. The telephone company charges 10 cents per minute for calls that last over 20 minutes. All other calls are 13 cents per minute. The telephone company also adds a $2 surcharge for calls outside the customer's area code. Take a few minutes to study the code that follows, and then answer Questions 1–4.

```
public class Exercise3_2
{
    public static void main(String args[])
    {
        int numMinutes;
        String outsideArea;
        double callCharge;
        numMinutes = 25;
        outsideArea = "Yes";
        if(numMinutes > 20)
            callCharge = numMinutes * .10;
        else
            callCharge = numMinutes * .13;
        if(outsideArea.equals("Yes"))
            callCharge += 2.00;
        System.out.println("The charge for this call is $" +
                            callCharge);
        System.exit(0);
    }
}
```

1. What is the exact output when this program executes?

    _____

    _____

2. What is the exact output if the value of **numMinutes** is changed to 13?

    _____

    _____

3. What is the exact output if the expression in the **if** statement is changed to
    numMinutes > 25?

    _____

    _____

4. What is the exact output if the variable named **outsideArea** is initialized with the value "No"
    rather than the value "Yes"?

    _____

    _____

LAB 3-2: USING IF ELSE STATEMENTS

In this lab, you complete a prewritten Java program that computes the largest of three integer values. The three values
are −10, 330, and 331.

1. Open the file named **Lab3_2.java** using Notepad or the text editor of your choice.
2. One variable named **largest** is declared for you. Use this variable to store the largest of the three
    integer values. You must decide what other variables you need and initialize them if appropriate.

3. Write the rest of the program using assignment statements, `if` statements, or `if else` statements as appropriate. There are comments in the code that tell you where you should write your statements. The output statement is written for you.

4. Compile the program.

5. Execute the program. Your output should be: The largest value is 331.

NESTED IF STATEMENTS

You can nest `if` statements to create a multipath decision statement. This is helpful in programs needing more than two paths to follow. Nesting an `if` statement means to include an `if` statement within an `if` statement.

The syntax, or rules, for writing a nested `if` statement in Java is as follows:

```
if(expressionA)
    statementA;
else if(expressionB)
    statementB;
else
    statementC;
```

TIP □ □ □ □ Do not include a semicolon at the end of the lines with expressions to be tested or on the line with the keyword `else`.

This is called a nested `if` statement because the second `if` statement is a part of the first `if` statement. This is easier to see if the example is changed as follows:

```
if(expressionA)
    statementA;
else
    if(expressionB)
        statementB;
    else
        statementC;
```

Now let's see how a nested `if` statement works. If *expressionA*, which is enclosed in parentheses, evaluates to `true`, then the computer will execute *statementA*. If *expressionA* evaluates to `false`, then the computer will evaluate *expressionB*. If *expressionB* evaluates to `true`, then the computer will execute *statementB*. If *expressionA* and *expressionB* both evaluate to `false`, then the computer will execute *statementC*. Regardless of which path is taken in this code, the statement following the `if else` statement is the next one to execute.

The Java code sample that follows illustrates a nested `if` statement:

```
if(empDept <= 3)
    supervisorName = "Dillon";
else if(empDept <= 7)
    supervisorName = "Escher";
else
    supervisorName = "Fontana";
System.out.println("Supervisor: " + supervisorName);
```

When you read the preceding code, you can assume that a department number is never less than 1. If the value of the variable named `empDept` is less than or equal to the value 3 (in the range of values from 1 to 3), then the value "`Dillon`" is assigned to the variable named `supervisorName`. If the value of `empDept` is not less than or equal to 3, but it is less than or equal to 7 (in the range of values from 4 to 7), then the value "`Escher`" is assigned to the variable named `supervisorName`. If the value of `empDept` is not in the range of values from 1 to 7, then the value "`Fontana`" is assigned to the variable named `supervisorName`. As you can see, there are three possible paths this program could take when the nested `if` statement is encountered. Regardless of which path the program takes, the next statement to execute is the output statement `System.out.println("Supervisor: " + supervisorName);`.

EXERCISE 3-3: UNDERSTANDING NESTED IF STATEMENTS

In this exercise, you use what you have learned about writing nested `if` statements in Java to study a complete Java program that uses nested `if` statements. This program was written for the Clip and Curl dog-grooming business to calculate a total charge for services rendered. Clip and Curl charges $20 for a bath, $25 for a trim, and $30 to clip nails. Take a few minutes to study the code that follows, and then answer Questions 1–3.

```
import javax.swing.*;
public class Exercise3_3
{
    public static void main(String args[])
    {
        String service;
        double charge;
        service =
            JOptionPane.showInputDialog("Enter service: ");
        if(service.equals("bath"))
            charge = 20.00;
        else if(service.equals("trim"))
            charge = 25.00;
        else if(service.equals("nail clip"))
            charge = 30.00;
        else
            charge = 0.00;
        if(charge > 0.00)
            System.out.println("The charge for a doggy " +
                                service + " is $" + charge);
```

```
        else
            System.out.println("We do not perform the " +
                                        service + " service.");
        System.exit(0);
    }
}
```

1. What is the exact output when this program executes if the user enters "bath"?

   _____

   _____

2. What is the exact output when this program executes if the user enters "shave"?

   _____

   _____

3. What is the exact output when this program executes if the user enters "bath" and the nested `if` statement is changed to `if(service == "bath")`?

   _____

   _____

LAB 3-3: USING NESTED IF STATEMENTS

In this lab, you complete a prewritten Java program that calculates an employee's end-of-year bonus and prints the employee's name, yearly salary, performance rating, and bonus. Bonuses are calculated based on an employee's annual salary and their performance rating. The rating system is as follows:

Rating	Bonus
1	6 percent of annual salary
2	4 percent of annual salary
3	2 percent of annual salary
4	None

1. Open the file named `Lab3_3.java` using Notepad or the text editor of your choice.
2. Variables have been declared for you and the input statements and output statements have been written. Read them over carefully before you proceed to the next step.
3. Design the logic and write the rest of the program using a nested `if` statement.
4. Compile the program.
5. Execute the program entering the following as input:

   Employee's name - **Frances Williams**

   Employee's salary - **45000.00**

   Employee's performance rating - **2**

6. Your output should be: Employee Name Frances Williams

Employee Salary $45000.0

Employee Rating 2

Employee Bonus $1800.0

TIP ◻ ◻ ◻ ◻ | You cannot control the number of places that appear after the decimal point until you learn more about Java.

USING DECISION STATEMENTS TO MAKE MULTIPLE COMPARISONS

When you write programs, you must often write statements that include multiple comparisons. For example, you may want to determine that two conditions are true before you decide which path your program will take. In the next sections, you learn how to implement AND logic in a program by using the `&&` (AND) logical operator. You also learn how to implement OR logic using the `||` (OR) logical operator.

USING AND LOGIC

When you write Java programs, you can use the AND operator `(&&)` to make multiple comparisons in a single decision statement. Remember when using AND logic that all expressions must evaluate to `true` for the entire expression to be true.

The Java code that follows illustrates a decision statement that uses the AND operator `(&&)` to implement AND logic:

```
String medicalPlan = "Y";
String dentalPlan = "Y";
if(medicalPlan.equals("Y") && dentalPlan.equals("Y"))
    System.out.println("Employee has medical insurance" +
                        " and also has dental insurance.");
else
    System.out.println("Employee may have medical" +
           " insurance or may have dental insurance," +
           " but does not have both medical and" +
           " dental insurance.");
```

In this example, the variables named `medicalPlan` and `dentalPlan` both have been initialized to the string constant `"Y"`. When the expression `medicalPlan.equals("Y")`, is evaluated, the result is `true`. When the expression `dentalPlan.equals("Y")` is evaluated, the result is also `true`. Because both expressions evaluate to `true`, the entire expression, `medicalPlan.equals("Y") && dentalPlan.equals("Y")`, evaluates to `true`. Because the entire expression is `true`, the output generated is `"Employee has medical insurance and also has dental insurance."`.

If you initialize either of the variables, `medicalPlan` or `dentalPlan`, with a value other than `"Y"`, then the expression `medicalPlan.equals("Y") && dentalPlan.equals("Y")` evaluates to `false`, and the output generated is "Employee may have medical insurance or may have dental insurance, but does not have both medical and dental insurance.".

USING OR LOGIC

You can use OR logic when you want to make multiple comparisons in a single decision statement. Of course, you must remember when using OR logic that only one expression must evaluate to true for the entire expression to be true.

The Java code that follows illustrates a decision statement that uses the OR operator (||) to implement OR logic:

```java
String medicalPlan = "Y";
String dentalPlan = "N";
if(medicalPlan.equals("Y") || dentalPlan.equals("Y"))
   System.out.println("Employee has medical insurance" +
        " or has dental insurance or has both medical" +
        " and dental insurance.");
else
   System.out.println("Employee does not have medical" +
        " insurance and also does not have dental" +
        " insurance.");
```

In this example, the variable named medicalPlan is initialized with the string constant "Y", and the variable named dentalPlan is initialized to the string constant "N". When the expression medicalPlan.equals("Y") is evaluated, the result is true. When the expression dentalPlan.equals("Y") is evaluated, the result is false. The expression, medicalPlan.equals("Y") || dentalPlan.equals("Y"), evaluates to true because when using OR logic, only one of the expressions must evaluate to true for the entire expression to be true. Because the entire expression is true, the output generated is "Employee has medical insurance or has dental insurance or has both medical and dental insurance.".

If you initialize both of the variables, medicalPlan and dentalPlan, with the string constant "N", then the expression, medicalPlan.equals("Y") || dentalPlan.equals("Y"), evaluates to false, and the output generated is "Employee does not have medical insurance and also does not have dental insurance.".

EXERCISE 3-4: MAKING MULTIPLE COMPARISONS IN DECISION STATEMENTS

In this exercise, you use what you have learned about OR logic to study a complete Java program that uses OR logic in a decision statement. This program was written for a college that wants to determine if a student is a French or Spanish major. Take a few minutes to study the code that follows, and then answer Questions 1–4.

```java
// Exercise3_4.java - This program determines if a
// student is a French or a Spanish major.
import javax.swing.*;
public class Lab3_4
{
   public static void main(String args[])
   {
     String studentName;   // Student's name.
     String major = "";     // Student's major.
     studentName = JOptionPane.showInputDialog(
        "Enter student's name: ");
     major = JOptionPane.showInputDialog(
        "Enter student's major: ");
     if(major.equals("French")||major.equals("Spanish"))
     {
        System.out.println("StudentName: " +
           studentName);
        System.out.println("Major: " + major);
     }
     else
        System.out.println(studentName +
           " is not a French or Spanish major.");
     System.exit(0);
   }
}
```

1. What is the exact output when this program executes if the student's name is Sudha Patel and the major is Spanish?

   _____

   _____

2. What is the exact output when this program executes if the student's name is Sudha Patel and the major is French?

   _____

   _____

3. What is the exact output from this program when

   ```
   if(major.equals("French") || major.equals("Spanish"))
   ```

   is changed to:

   ```
   if(major.equals("French") && major.equals("Spanish"))
   ```

   and the student's name is still Sudha Patel and the major is still Spanish?

   _____

   _____

4. What is the exact output from this program when

```
if(major.equals("French") || major.equals("Spanish"))
```

is changed to

```
if(major.equals("French") || major.equals("Spanish") ||
major.equals("french") || major.equals("spanish"))
```

and the student's name is Sudha Patel, and the major is French? What does this change allow a user to enter?

_____

_____

LAB 3-4: MAKING MULTIPLE COMPARISONS IN DECISION STATEMENTS

In this lab, you complete a prewritten Java program that is written for a candy company. The company wants to know if a candy is a best-selling item and also a high-priced item. Best-selling items sell over 2,000 pounds per month. High-priced items sell for $10 or more per pound.

1. Open the file named `Lab3_4.java` using Notepad or the text editor of your choice.
2. Variables have been declared for you, and the input statements have been written. Read them carefully before you proceed to the next step.
3. Design the logic deciding whether to use AND or OR logic. Write the decision statement to identify both high-priced and best-selling candy.
4. Be sure to include output statements telling whether this is a high-priced, best-selling item.
5. Compile the program.
6. Execute the program, entering the following as input:
   a. Candy name: `Turtles`

      Price per pound: `22.00`

      Quantity sold: `2100`

      What is the output? _____

      _____

   b. Candy name: `Nougats`

      Price per pound: `12.00`

      Quantity sold: `2100`

      What is the output? _____

      _____

c. Candy name: `Gummi Bears`

Price per pound: `2.00`

Quantity sold: `5000`

What is the output? _____

_____

d. Candy name: `Chocolate Raisins`

Price per pound: `20.50`

Quantity sold: `2000`

What is the output? _____

_____

e. Candy name: `SloPokes`

Price per pound: `2.00`

Quantity sold: `6100`

What is the output? _____

_____

f. Candy name: `Truffles`

Price per pound: `27.00`

Quantity sold: `2005`

What is the output? _____

_____

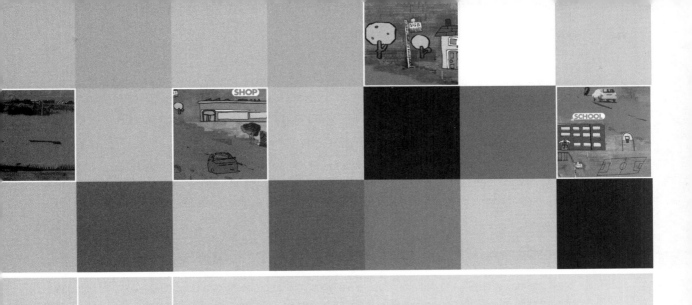

4

WRITING PROGRAMS USING LOOPS

After studying Chapter 4, you will be able to:

- ☐ Use Java's increment (++) and decrement (--) operators
- ☐ Recognize how and when to use **while** loops in Java, including using a counter, using a sentinel value, and using an event to control a loop
- ☐ Use **for** loops in Java
- ☐ Write a **do while** loop in Java
- ☐ Include nested loops in programs
- ☐ Accumulate totals by using loops in a program

In this chapter, you learn how to use Java to program three types of loops: a `while` loop, a `do while` loop, and a `for` loop. You also learn how to nest loops and how to use a loop to help you accumulate a total in your programs. But before you start learning about Java's loops, it is helpful for you to learn about two additional operators, the increment and decrement operators.

It is recommended that you do the exercises and labs in this chapter only after you have finished Chapter 6 of your book, *Programming Logic and Design*. In Chapter 6 you learned that loops change the flow of control in a program by allowing a programmer to direct the computer to execute a statement or a group of statements multiple times.

THE INCREMENT (++) AND DECREMENT (--) OPERATORS

You often use the increment and decrement operators when your programs require loops. These operators provide a concise, efficient method for adding 1 to (incrementing) or subtracting 1 from (decrementing) an lvalue. An **lvalue** is an area of memory in which values your programs need may be stored. An lvalue must be placed on the left side of an assignment statement. Recall that an assignment statement stores a value at a memory location that is associated with a variable, and you place a variable name on the left side of an assignment statement.

TIP □ □ □ □ | The "l" in "lvalue" represents "left."

For example, the Java assignment statement:

```
number = 10;
```

assigns the value `10` to the variable named `number`. This causes the computer to store the value `10` at the memory location associated with `number`. Because the increment and decrement operators add 1 to or subtract 1 from an lvalue, the statement `number++;` is equivalent to `number = number + 1;`, and the statement `number--;` is equivalent to `number = number - 1;`. Each expression in these statements changes or writes to the memory location associated with the variable named `number`.

Both the increment and decrement operators have prefix and postfix forms. Which form you use depends on when you want the value of the variable to be incremented or decremented. When you use the **prefix form**, as in `++number`, you place the operator in front of the name of the variable. This causes the lvalue to be incremented or decremented immediately. When you use the **postfix form**, as in `number++`, you place the operator after the name of the variable. This causes the lvalue to be incremented or decremented after it is used.

The example that follows illustrates the use of both forms of the increment operator in Java:

```
x = 5;
y = x++;   // Postfix form -- y is assigned the value
           // of x, then x is incremented.
           // Value of x is 6.
           // Value of y is 5.
```

```
x = 5;
y = ++x;   // Prefix form -- x is incremented first,
           // then the value of x is assigned to y.
           // Value of x is 6.
           // Value of y is 6.
```

You might understand the postfix form better if you think of the statement x++; as being the same as the following:

```
x = 5;
y = x;
x = x + 1;
```

You might understand the prefix form better if you think of ++x; as being the same as the following:

```
x = 5;
x = x + 1;
y = x;
```

EXERCISE 4-1: USING THE INCREMENT AND DECREMENT OPERATORS

In this exercise, you examine code and use what you have learned about Java's increment and decrement operators to answer the related questions.

1. Examine the following code:

```
a = 3;
b = ++a;
```

   What is the value of a? _____ b? _____

2. Examine the following code:

```
a = 3;
b = a++;
```

   What is the value of a? _____ b? _____

3. Examine the following code:

```
a = 3;
b = --a;
```

   What is the value of a? _____ b? _____

4. Examine the following code:

```
a = 3;
b = a--;
```

   What is the value of a? _____ b? _____

WRITING A WHILE LOOP IN JAVA

As you learned in *Programming Logic and Design*, there are three steps that must occur in every loop:

1. You must initialize a variable that will control the loop. This variable is known as the **loop control variable**.
2. You must compare the loop control variable to some value, known as the **sentinel value,** which decides whether the loop continues or stops. This decision is based on a Boolean comparison. The result of a **Boolean** comparison is always a true or false value.
3. Within the loop, you must alter the loop control variable.

You also learned that the statements that are part of a loop are referred to as the **loop body**. In Java, the loop body may consist of a single statement or a block statement.

TIP ▫ ▫ ▫ ▫ | Remember that a block statement is several statements within a pair of curly braces.

The statements that make up the loop body may be any type of statement, including assignment statements, decision statements, or even other loops. Note that the Java syntax for writing a `while` loop is as follows:

```
while(expression)
    statement;
```

Notice that there is no semicolon after the ending parenthesis. Placing a semicolon after the ending parenthesis is not a syntax error, but it is a logic error. It results in an **infinite** loop, which is a loop that never stops executing the statements in its body. It never stops executing because the semicolon is a statement called the **null** statement and is interpreted as "do nothing." Think of a while loop with a semicolon after the ending parenthesis as meaning "while the condition is true, do nothing forever."

The `while` loop allows you to direct the computer to execute the statement in the body of the loop as long as the expression within the parentheses evaluates to true. Study the example that follows. This example illustrates a `while` loop with a single statement in the loop body.

```
num = 0;
while(num++ < 3)
    System.out.println("Welcome to Java Programming.");
```

In the preceding example, the loop body includes one statement that executes three times, which causes the text "Welcome to Java Programming." to appear on the user's screen three times. Be sure you understand why the postfix increment operator is used in the expression `num++ < 3`. The first time this comparison is made, the value of `num` is 0. The 0 is then compared to, and found to be less than, 3, which means the condition is true, and the text "Welcome to Java Programming." is displayed.

TIP ▫ ▫ ▫ ▫ | Remember that the value of `num` is not incremented until after the comparison is done.

The second time the comparison is made, the value of `num` is 1, which is still less than 3, causing the sentence to appear a second time. The third comparison also results in a true value because the value of `num` is now 2, and 2 is still less than 3.

If the prefix increment operator is used in the expression `++num < 3`, the loop executes twice instead of three times. This occurs because the first time this comparison is evaluated, `num` is incremented before the comparison is done. This results in `num` having a value of 1 the first time "Welcome to Java Programming." is displayed and a value of 2 the second time it is displayed. Then, when the value of `num` is 3, the condition is false, causing your program to exit the loop and "Welcome to Java Programming." not to be displayed the third time.

TIP ▫ ▫ ▫ ▫ | It is important to understand the difference between the prefix and postfix forms of the increment and decrement operators.

The next example illustrates a `while` loop that uses a block statement as its loop body:

```
num = 0;
while(num < 3)
{
        System.out.println("Welcome to Java Programming.");
        num++;
}
```

This loop produces the same results as the previous example. The sentence "Welcome to Java Programming." is displayed three times. As you can see, the difference is that a second statement, `num++`, was added to the loop body, a block statement is used because now there is more than one statement in the loop body, and the increment operator is not used in the Boolean expression controlling the loop. There is no need to use the increment operator in the Boolean expression because the increment is now done in the loop body.

TIP ▫ ▫ ▫ ▫ | Most people think that the loop using the block statement is better because it is easier to read and understand.

EXERCISE 4-2: USING A WHILE LOOP

In this exercise, you use what you have learned about writing `while` loops to study the following code and then answer the subsequent questions.

First, study the Java code:

```
count = 10;
while(count++ < 10)
    System.out.println("Value of count is " + count);
```

1. What is the loop control variable?

    _____

2. What is the output?

    _____

3. What is the output if the code is changed to `while(count++ <= 10)`?

    _____

4. What is the output if the code is change to `while(++count <= 10)`?

    _____

USING A COUNTER TO CONTROL A LOOP

In Chapter 6 of *Programming Logic and Design*, you learned that you can use a counter to control a `while` loop. With a counter, you set up the loop to execute a specified number of times. Also recall that a `while` loop may execute zero times if the expression used in the comparison immediately evaluates to false. In that case, the computer does not execute the body of the loop at all.

Chapter 6 of the *Programming Logic and Design* book also discusses two loops: one is controlled by an event and a counter controls the other. The counter-controlled loop also controls how many labels are printed. Let's look at the pseudocode for this counter-controlled loop, as follows:

```
labelCounter = 0
while labelCounter < 100
    print labelLine, firstName
    labelCounter = labelCounter + 1
endWhile
```

The counter for this counter-controlled loop is a variable named `labelCounter`, which is assigned the value 0. The Boolean expression, `labelCounter < 100`, is tested to see if the value of `labelCounter` is less than 100. If true, the loop executes. If false, the program exits the loop. If the loop executes, the program prints the contents of the variable named `labelLine` followed by the value of the variable named `firstName`, and then adds 1 to the value of `labelCounter`. Given this pseudocode, the loop body should execute 100 times and 100 labels should be printed.

Now, let's see what the code looks like when you translate the pseudocode to Java:

```
labelCounter = 0;
while(labelCounter < 100)
{
    System.out.println(labelLine + firstName);
    labelCounter++;
}
```

First, the variable `labelCounter` is assigned a value of 0 and is used as the counter variable to control the `while` loop. The `while` loop follows and includes the Boolean expression, `labelCounter < 100`, within parentheses. The counter-controlled loop executes a block statement that is marked by an opening curly brace and a closing curly brace. The statements in the loop body display the value of `labelLine` followed by the value of `firstName`. Then the `labelCounter` variable is incremented, which adds 1 to the counter variable.

TIP □ □ □ □ Incrementing the counter variable is an important statement. Each time through the loop, the `labelCounter` variable must be incremented or the expression `labelCounter < 100` would never be false. This would result in an **infinite** loop.

EXERCISE 4-3: USING A COUNTER-CONTROLLED WHILE LOOP

In this exercise, you use what you have learned about counter-controlled loops to study the following Java code, and then answer questions about the code.

```
num1 = 0;
num2 = 0;
while(num1 < 10)
    num1++;
    num2 += num1;
```

1. What is the value of `num1` when the loop exits? _____

2. What is the value of `num2` when the loop exits? _____

3. If the statement `num1++` is changed to `++num1`, what is the value of `num1` when the loop exits?

   _____

4. What could you do to force the value of `num2` to be 55 when the loop exits?

   _____

LAB 4-1: USING A COUNTER-CONTROLLED WHILE LOOP

In this lab, you use a counter-controlled `while` loop in a partially prewritten Java program. The program is written to print the numbers 0 through 10, along with their squares and cubes. Variables have been declared and output statements have been written for you.

1. Open the source code file named `Square_Cube.java` using Notepad or the text editor of your choice.

2. Write a counter-controlled `while` loop that uses the loop control variable to take on the values 0 through 10. Remember to initialize the loop control variable before the loop is entered.

3. In the body of the loop, calculate the square and the cube using the value of the loop control variable. Remember to change the value of the loop control variable in the body of the loop.

4. Save this source code file in a directory of your choice and then make that directory your working directory.

5. Compile the source code file, `Square_Cube.java`.

6. Execute the program. Record the output of this program.

_____

_____

USING A SENTINEL VALUE TO CONTROL A LOOP

For this example, a few changes are made to the label-printing program you saw in the previous section. Now, as discussed in _Programming Logic and Design_, instead of printing 100 labels for each employee, you have decided to print enough labels to cover 110% of each employee's production rate from the previous week. The pseudocode has been rewritten to handle this change:

```
labelCounter = 0
labelsToPrint = inLastProduction * 1.1
while labelCounter < labelsToPrint
    print labelLine, firstName
    labelCounter = labelCounter + 1
end while
```

As you can see, the original pseudocode was modified to accommodate the changes you want to make in your program. Now, you can calculate the number of labels to print and use this calculated value as your loop control variable rather than the constant value of 100 you used before.

You can see the modified pseudocode translated to Java in the following code sample:

```
labelCounter = 0;
labelsToPrint = inLastProduction * 1.1;
while(labelCounter < labelsToPrint)
{
    System.out.println(labelLine + firstName);
    labelCounter++;
}
```

This code is different from the Java code shown in the previous section. The statement `labelsToPrint = inLastProduction * 1.1;` has been added to calculate the number of labels to print. Note that in addition to the calculation, you also need to change the Boolean expression used to control the `while` loop, as shown:

```
while(labelCounter < labelsToPrint)
```

Now, your code would use the calculated number of labels to print, `labelsToPrint`, instead of always printing 100 labels.

EXERCISE 4-4: USING A SENTINEL VALUE TO CONTROL A WHILE LOOP

In this exercise, you use what you have learned about using a sentinel value to control a `while` loop to study the Java code that follows, and then answer the subsequent questions.

```java
stringNum = JOptionPane.showInputDialog(
    "How many labels do you want to print?");
numToPrint = Integer.parseInt(stringNum);
counter = 1;
while(counter < numToPrint);
{
    System.out.println("Label Number " + counter);
    counter++;
}
System.out.println("Value of counter is " + counter);
```

1. What is the output?

2. If you think there is a problem with this code, what must you do to fix it?

3. Assume that you fixed the problem in Question 2. Now, if the user enters 150 as the number of labels to print, what is the value of **counter** when the loop exits?

4. Assume that you fixed the problem in Question 2. Now, if the user enters 0 as the number of labels to print, how many labels will print?

5. What is the output if the curly braces are deleted?

LAB 4-2: USING A SENTINEL VALUE TO CONTROL A WHILE LOOP

In this lab, you write a `while` loop that uses a sentinel value to control a loop in a partially prewritten Java program. You also write the statements that make up the body of the loop. Variables have been declared and input and output statements have been written for you. The program is written to print a payoff schedule for a credit card company customer. This is the same problem described in Exercise 4 of Chapter 6 in *Programming Logic and Design*, except that it calculates a payoff schedule for only one customer. You will see that this program generates a lot of output even for one customer. Also, at the beginning of every month, 1.5% interest is added to the balance, and then the customer makes a payment equal to 5% of the current balance. When the balance reaches $10.00 or less, the customer can pay off the account.

1. Open the source code file named **CreditCard.java** using Notepad or the text editor of your choice.

2. Write the `while` loop using a sentinel value to control the loop, and also write the statements that make up the body of the loop.

3. Save this source code file in a directory of your choice, and then make that directory your working directory.

4. Compile the source code file, `CreditCard.java`.

5. Execute the program. Input the following:

   Account Number: `1234A`

   Customer Name: `Maria Sanchez`

   Balance: `150.00`

6. Record the final balance amount when the loan may be paid off.

USING AN EVENT TO CONTROL A LOOP

You can also use an event to help you control a `while` loop in a program. You want to use this method when you don't know how many times you are required to repeat the statements in a loop. Instead, you use an event to alert you when to stop the loop. An **event** could be reaching the end of the file your program is using for input, or it could be a signal from the user of your program that he or she wants to stop the action being carried out in the loop.

Because reading input from a file is beyond your abilities in Java, we use a signal from the user of your program as an example of an event-controlled loop. Suppose you want to write a program to determine the letter grade associated with a numeric score your students have earned on their midterm exam. You would write the following pseudocode:

```
read studentName
while studentName <> "done"
   read studentScore
   if studentScore >= 90
      letterGrade = "A"
   else if studentScore >= 80
      letterGrade = "B"
   else if studentScore >= 70
      letterGrade = "C"
   else if studentScore >= 60
      letterGrade = "D"
   else
      letterGrade = "F"
   print studentName, letterGrade
   read studentName
endWhile
```

Note that a priming read has been used in the design in the preceding code. As you learned in Chapter 2 of *Programming Logic and Design*, a **priming read** is performed before a loop is entered to get a value that is used to control the loop. You also learned that when a priming read is used, you must perform the same read action as the last statement in the loop to get the next value. The priming read is needed in the preceding program because your design has the user providing input to the program. The input is each student's name and a numeric test score. When all of the student names and scores have been entered, the user enters the word "done" instead of a student name. This event will cause an exit from the loop.

The Java code that follows shows this event-controlled loop, along with the priming read. The entire Java program is saved in a file named `StudentGrades.java`. You may want to study the source code, compile it, and execute the program to experience how an event-controlled loop behaves.

```java
studentName = JOptionPane.showInputDialog(
    "Enter student's  name: ");
while(studentName.compareTo("done") != 0)
{
    studentScore = JOptionPane.showInputDialog(
        "Enter student's numeric score: ");
    numericScore = Integer.parseInt(studentScore);
    if(numericScore >= 90)
        letterGrade = "A";
    else if(numericScore >= 80)
        letterGrade = "B";
    else if(numericScore >= 70)
        letterGrade = "C";
    else if(numericScore >= 60)
        letterGrade = "D";
    else
        letterGrade = "F";
    System.out.println(studentName + " received a(n) " +
        letterGrade);
    studentName=JOptionPane.showInputDialog(
        "Enter student's name:");
}
```

EXERCISE 4-5: USING AN EVENT TO CONTROL A WHILE LOOP

In this exercise, you use what you have learned about controlling `while` loops using an event to study the Java code that follows, and then answer the subsequent questions. The code is part of a program used to calculate daily book sales.

```java
String stringPrice;
double price;
String bookTitle;
double total = 0.0;
```

```
stringPrice = JOptionPane.showInputDialog(
   "Enter price or 0 to quit.");
price = Double.parseDouble(stringPrice);
while(price != 0.0)
{
   bookTitle = JOptionPane.showInputDialog(
      "Enter book title: ");
   System.out.println("Title: " + bookTitle + "Price: $"
      + price);
   total += price;
}
System.out.println("Total for all books is: $" + total);
```

1. What event controls this loop?

   _____

2. Will the loop execute correctly?

   _____

3. If there is a problem, what must be done to correct it?

   _____

4. What is the result if `total += price;` is changed to `total = price;`?

   _____

LAB 4-3: USING AN EVENT TO CONTROL A WHILE LOOP

In this lab, you use an event to control a `while` loop in a partially prewritten Java program. The program is a guessing game. A random number between 1 and 10 is generated in the program. The user of the program enters a number between 1 and 10, trying to guess the correct number. If the user guesses correctly, you exit the loop that controls guessing numbers; otherwise, you ask the user if he or she wants to guess again. If he or she enters a "Y", you allow a second guess. If he or she enters "N", you exit the loop. You can see that the user entering a "Y" or a "N" is the event that controls your loop. Note that in this program, variables have been declared, a random number is generated, and the input and output statements have been written for you.

1. Open the source code file named `GuessNumber.java` using Notepad or the text editor of your choice.
2. Write an event-controlled loop that executes if the user enters a "Y" when asked if he or she wants to guess a number. Notice the prewritten statement that primes the loop.
3. Within the loop, test to see if the number your user guessed is correct.
4. Save this source code file in a directory of your choice, and then make that directory your working directory.

5. Compile the source code file, `GuessNumber.java`.

6. Execute the program. See if you can guess the randomly generated number. Execute the program several times to see if the random number changes.

WRITING A FOR LOOP IN JAVA

In Chapter 6 of *Programming Logic and Design*, you learned that a `for` loop is a **definite** loop; this means this type of loop executes a definite number of times. The following is the syntax for writing a `for` loop in Java:

```
for(expression1; expression2; expression3)
    statement;
```

In Java, the `for` loop consists of three expressions that are separated by semicolons and enclosed within parentheses. The `for` loop executes as follows:

1. The first time the `for` loop is encountered, the first expression is evaluated. Usually, this expression initializes a variable that is used to control the `for` loop.

2. Next, the second expression is evaluated. If the second expression evaluates to true, the loop statement executes. If the second expression evaluates to false, the loop is exited.

3. After the loop statement executes, the third expression is evaluated. The third expression usually increments or decrements the variable that you initialized in the first expression.

4. After the third expression is evaluated, the second expression is evaluated again. If the second expression still evaluates to true, the loop statement executes again, and then the third expression is evaluated again.

5. This process continues until the second expression evaluates to false.

The following code sample illustrates a Java `for` loop. Notice that the code·uses a block statement in the `for` loop, just as it does in a `while` loop.

```
int number = 0;
for(count = 0; count < 10; count++)
{
    number += count;
    System.out.println("Value of number is: " + number);
}
```

In this `for` loop example, the variable named `count` is initialized to `0` in the first expression. The second expression is a Boolean expression that evaluates to true or false. When the expression `count < 10` is evaluated the first time, the value of `count` is `0` and the result is true. The loop body is then entered. This is where a new value is computed and assigned to the variable named `number` and then is displayed. The first time through the loop, the output is as follows: `Value of number is: 0`.

After the output is displayed, the third expression in the `for` loop is evaluated, which adds 1 to the value of `count`. The new value of `count` is 1. Expression two is evaluated a second time. The value of `count`, 1, is tested to see if it is less than 10. This results in a true value and causes the loop body to execute again. A new value is computed for `number` and then displayed. The second time through the loop, the output is as follows: `Value of number is: 1`.

Next, expression three is evaluated, which adds 1 to the value of `count`. The value of `count` is now 2. Expression two is evaluated a third time and again is true because 2 is less than 10. The third time through the loop body changes the value of `number` to 3 and then displays the new value. The output is as follows: `Value of number is: 3`.

This process continues until the value of `count` becomes 10. At this time, 10 is not less than 10, so the second expression results in a false value. This causes an exit from the `for` loop.

The counter-controlled loop you studied in the "Using A Counter To Control A Loop" section of this chapter can be rewritten using a `for` loop instead of the `while` loop. In fact, when you know how many times a loop will execute, it is considered a good programming practice to use a `for` loop.

To rewrite the `while` loop as a `for` loop, you can delete the assignment statement, `labelCounter = 0;`, because you will initialize `labelCounter` in expression one. You can also delete `labelCounter++;` from the loop body because you will increment `labelCounter` in expression three. You continue to print the label in the body of the loop. The following code sample illustrates this `for` loop:

```
for(labelCounter = 0; labelCounter < 100; labelCounter++)
    System.out.println(labelLine + firstName);
```

TIP ▫ ▫ ▫ ▫ | The curly braces have also been removed because now there is just one statement in the body of the loop.

EXERCISE 4-6: USING A FOR LOOP

In this exercise, you use what you have learned about `for` loops to study the Java code that follows and answer the subsequent questions:

```
for(num = 1; num <= 12; num++)
{
    System.out.println("Value of num is: " + num);
    num++;
}
```

Answer the following four questions by writing True or False.

1. This loop executes twelve times. _____
2. This loop could be written as a `while` loop. _____
3. Changing the <= operator to < makes no difference in the output. _____
4. This loop executes six times. _____

LAB 4-4: USING A FOR LOOP

In this lab, you rewrite a Java program that uses a counter-controlled `while` loop. The program generates a listing of the squares and cubes of the numbers 0 through 10. This is the same program with which you worked in Lab 4-1, except that you will replace the counter-controlled `while` loop with a `for` loop.

1. Open the source code file named `New_Square_Cube.java` using Notepad or the text editor of your choice.
2. Comment out the statements that are part of the counter-controlled `while` loop.
3. Replace the counter-controlled `while` loop with a `for` loop.
4. Save this source code file in a directory of your choice, and then make that directory your working directory.
5. Compile the source code file, `New_Square_Cube.java`.
6. Execute the program. Is the output the same?

WRITING A DO WHILE LOOP IN JAVA

In Chapter 6 of *Programming Logic and Design*, you learned about the `do until` loop. Java does not support a `do until` loop, but it does have a `do while` loop. The `do while` loop uses logic that can be stated as "do *a* while *b* is true." This is the same as a `while` loop, except that the condition is tested after the `do while` loop body executes once. As a result, you will choose a `do while` loop when your program logic requires the body of the loop to always execute at least once. The body of a `do while` loop continues to execute as long as the expression evaluates to true. The `do while` syntax is as follows:

```
do
    statement;
while(expression);
```

The code sample that follows illustrates the `while` loop that prints 100 labels rewritten as a `do while` loop.

```
labelCounter = 0;
do
{
    if(labelCounter < 100)
    {
        System.out.println(labelLine + firstName);
        labelCounter++;
    }
}while(labelCounter < 100);
```

To rewrite the loop, you use an `if` statement to immediately test whether you have printed all of the 100 labels. You do this because when you use the `do while` loop, the condition (`labelCounter < 100`) is not tested until the end of the loop. If you have not printed 100 labels, you continue with the work of the loop. If you have printed 100 labels, you do not want to continue. Notice that you use block statements in `do while` loops just as you do in `while` and `for` loops.

EXERCISE 4-7: USING A DO WHILE LOOP

In this exercise, you use what you have learned about `do while` loops in Java to study the code that follows and answer the subsequent questions.

```
numTimes = 3;
counter = 0;
do
{
   counter++;
   System.out.println("Strike " + counter);
}while(counter < numTimes);
```

1. How many times does this loop execute?

2. What is the output of this program?

3. Is the output different if you change the order of the statements in the body of loop, so that `counter++` comes after the output statement?

4. What is the loop control variable?

LAB 4-5: USING A DO WHILE LOOP

In this lab, you rewrite a Java program that uses a counter-controlled `while` loop. You replace the counter-controlled `while` loop with a `do while` loop. The program generates a listing of the squares and cubes of the numbers 0 through 10. This is the same program with which you worked in Lab 4-1 and Lab 4-4. This program shows you that a single problem can be solved in different ways.

1. Open the source code file named `Newest_Square_Cube.java` using Notepad or the text editor of your choice.
2. Comment out the statements that are part of the counter-controlled `while` loop.
3. Replace the counter-controlled `while` loop with a `do while` loop.
4. Save this source code file in a directory of your choice and then make that directory your working directory.

5. Compile the source code file, `Newest_Square_Cube.java`.

6. Execute the program. Is the output the same?

NESTING LOOPS

As your programs become more complex, you may find that a nested loop is required as part of your logic design. This means that you may need to include a loop within another loop. You have learned that when you use nested loops in a program, you must use multiple control variables to control the separate loops.

In *Programming Logic and Design*, you studied the design logic to produce a Projected Payroll report. For each employee of a company, the program computes a one-fourth of one percent raise for each pay period during the coming year. The employees in this company are paid twice per month. A section of the pseudocode for this program is as follows:

```
monthCounter = 1
while monthCounter <= numberOfMonthsInYear
   checkCounter = 1
   while checkCounter <= numberOfChecksInMonth
      weekSal = weekSal + weekSal * raiseRate
      print monthCounter, checkCounter, weekSal
      checkCounter = checkCounter + 1
   endWhile
   monthCounter = monthCounter + 1
endWhile
```

By studying the pseudocode, you can see that there are two loops. The outer loop uses the loop control variable named `monthCounter` to keep track of the month (1 through 12). The inner loop uses the control variable `checkCounter` to keep track of the pay period in the month (1 through 2). Refer to *Programming Logic and Design* for a line-by-line description of the pseudocode. When you are sure you understand the logic, look at the code sample that follows. This code sample shows some of the Java code for the Projected Payroll Report program.

```java
// Initialize month to 1.
monthCounter = 1;
// Loop for each month in the year.
while(monthCounter <= numberOfMonthsInYear)
{
   // Initialize counter each time before inner loop.
   checkCounter = 1;
   // Loop for each pay period.
```

```
        while(checkCounter <= 2)
        {
            // Calculate pay raise.
            weekSal = weekSal + weekSal * raiseRate;
            // One more space in output for months 1-9.
            if(monthCounter < 10)
                System.out.println(monthCounter + "      "
                       + checkCounter + "        $" + weekSal);
            else
                System.out.println(monthCounter + "      "
                       + checkCounter + "        $" + weekSal);
            // Next pay period.
            checkCounter++;
        }
        // Next month.
        monthCounter++;

    }
```

The entire Java program is saved in a file named `ProjectedPayroll.java`. You may want to study the source code, compile it, and execute the program to experience how nested loops behave.

EXERCISE 4-8: NESTING LOOPS

In this exercise, you use what you learned about nesting loops in Java to study the code that follows, and then answer the subsequent questions.

```
int sum = 0, max_rows = 5, max_cols = 4;
int rows, columns;
for(rows = 0; rows < max_rows; rows++)
    for(columns = 0; columns < max_cols; columns++)
        sum += rows + columns;
System.out.println("Value of sum is " + sum);
```

1. How many times does the outer loop execute?

    _____

2. How many times does the inner loop execute?

    _____

3. What is the value of `sum` printed by `System.out.println()`?

    _____

4. What would happen if you changed `rows++` and `columns++` to `++rows` and `++columns`?

    _____

LAB 4-6: NESTING LOOPS

In this lab, you add nested loops to a partially prewritten Java program. The program should print the outline of a rectangle that looks like the rectangle shown in Figure 4-1. The rectangle is printed using asterisks, 10 across and 12 down. This program uses `System.out.print("*");` to print an asterisk without a new line.

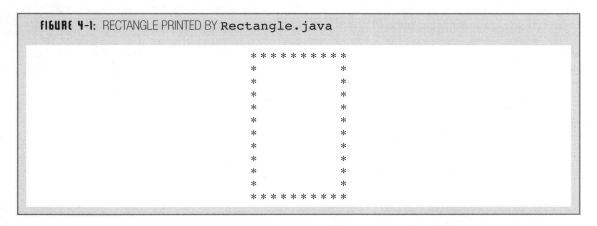

FIGURE 4-1: RECTANGLE PRINTED BY `Rectangle.java`

1. Open the source code file named `Rectangle.java` using Notepad or the text editor of your choice.
2. Write the nested loops to control the number of rows and the number of columns that make up the rectangle.
3. In the loop body, use a nested `if` statement to decide when to print an asterisk and when to print a space. The output statements have been written, but you must decide when and where to use them.
4. Save this source code file in a directory of your choice, and then make that directory your working directory.
5. Compile the source code file, `Rectangle.java`.
6. Execute the program. Your rectangle outline should look like the rectangle outline in Figure 4-1.

ACCUMULATING TOTALS IN A LOOP

As a Java programmer, you can use loops to accumulate totals as your programs execute. For example, assume that your computer science instructor asks you to design and write a program that she can use to calculate an average score for the midterm exam she gave last week. To find the average test score, you need to add all of the students' test scores, and then divide that sum by the number of students who took the midterm.

Note that the logic for this program should include a loop that will execute for each student in the class. In the loop, you get a student's test score as input and add that value to a total. After you get all of the test scores and accumulate the sum of all the test scores, you will divide that sum by the number of students. You should plan to ask the user to input the number of student test scores that will be entered, because your instructor wants to reuse this program using a different number of students each time it is executed.

As you review your work, you realize that you will accumulate a sum within the loop and you will also need to keep a count for the number of students. You learned in *Programming Logic and Design* that you add one to a counter each time a loop executes and that you add some other value to an accumulator. For this program, that other value added to the accumulator is a student's test score.

The following Java code sample shows the loop required for this program, as well as the use of an accumulator and a counter in the loop body:

```java
// Get user input to control loop.
stringNum = JOptionPane.showInputDialog(
   "Enter number of students: ");
// Convert number String to int.
numStudents = Integer.parseInt(stringNum);
// Initialize accumulator variable to 0.
testTotal = 0;
// Loop for each student.
for(stuCount = 0; stuCount < numStudents; stuCount++)
{
   // Input student test score.
   stringScore = JOptionPane.showInputDialog(
      "Enter student's score: ");
   // Convert to integer.
   testScore = Integer.parseInt(stringScore);
   // Accumulate total of test scores.
   testTotal += testScore;
}
// Calculate average test score.
average = testTotal / stuCount;
```

In the code, you use the `showInputDialog()` method to ask your user to tell you how many students took the test. Then you convert the `String` value that is returned by the `showInputDialog()` method to an `int` so that you can use the value in arithmetic calculations. Next, the accumulator, `testTotal`, is initialized to `0`.

TIP □ □ □ □ If `testTotal` is not initialized, it will contain an unknown value referred to as a "garbage" value. In Java, your program will not compile if `testTotal` is not initialized.

After the accumulator is initialized, the code uses a `for` loop and the loop control variable, `stuCount`, to control the loop. A `for` loop is a good choice because, at this point in the program, you know how many times the loop should execute. You use the `for` loop's first expression to initialize `stuCount`, and then the second expression is evaluated to see if `stuCount` is less than `numStudents`. If this is true, the body of the loop executes where you use the `showInputDialog()` method again, this time to ask the user to enter a test score.

As you continue to examine the code, note that because the `showInputDialog()` method returns the `String` version of the value entered by your user, you must convert this `String` to an `int` by using the `parseInt()` method. Then, you add the value of `testScore` to the accumulator, `testTotal`. The loop control variable, `stuCount`, is then incremented, and the incremented value is tested to see if it is less than `numStudents`. If this is true again, the loop executes a second time. The loop continues to execute until the value of `stuCount < numStudents` is false. Outside the `for` loop, you calculate the average test score by dividing `testTotal` by `stuCount`.

TIP ☐ ☐ ☐ ☐ Calculating the average must be done outside the loop, not inside the loop. If you calculate the average inside the loop, it is done each time the loop executes, which is not what you want to have happen.

The entire Java program is saved in a file named `TestAverage.java`. You may want to study the source code, compile it, and execute the program to experience how accumulators and counters behave.

EXERCISE 4-9: ACCUMULATING TOTALS IN A LOOP

In this exercise, you use what you have learned about using counters and accumulating totals in a loop. Study the Java code that follows, and then answer the subsequent questions about the code. The complete program is saved in the file named `Temperature.java`. You may want to compile and execute the program to help you answer these questions.

```java
for(counter = 1; counter <= 7; counter++)
{
    stringTemp = JOptionPane.showInputDialog(
        "Enter temperature for Day " + counter);
    temperature = Double.parseDouble(stringTemp);
    System.out.println("Day " + counter +
        " temperature is " + temperature);
    sum += temperature;
}
// Calculate average.
average = sum / 7;
```

1. What happens when you compile this program if the variable `sum` is not initialized with the value 0?

_____

2. Could you replace `sum += temperature;` with `sum = sum + temperature;`?

_____

3. The variables `sum` and `average` should be declared to be what data type to calculate the most accurate average temperature?

_____

4. Could you replace the 7 in the statement `average = sum / 7;` with the variable named `counter` and still get the desired result? Explain.

_____

_____

LAB 4-7: ACCUMULATING TOTALS IN A LOOP

In this lab, you add a loop and the statements that make up the loop body to a prewritten Java program. The program is written to calculate the total of your monthly bills. Your loop should execute until your user enters the word "done" instead of a bill type. After your user enters a bill type, he or she should be asked to enter the bill amount. Your bills are listed in Table 4-1.

TABLE 4-1: INPUT FOR LAB 4-7

Bill Type	Bill Amount
Rent	$800.00
Car Payment	$550.00
Car Insurance	$100.00
Food	$400.00
Gasoline	$120.00
Utilities	$275.00
Miscellaneous	$125.00

Note that variables have been declared for you and the input and output statements have been written, but you must decide where they belong in the program.

1. Open the source code file named **MonthlyBills.java** using Notepad or the text editor of your choice.
2. Write your loop and the loop body that allows you to calculate a total of your monthly bills.
3. Save this source code file in a directory of your choice, and then make that directory your working directory.
4. Compile the source code file, **MonthlyBills.java**.
5. Execute the program using the data listed in Table 4-1. Record the output of this program.

   _____

   _____

   _____

   _____

5

WRITING CONTROL BREAK PROGRAMS AND READING DATA FROM INPUT FILES

After studying Chapter 5, you will be able to:

☐ Read data from files

☐ Understand how to accumulate totals in single-level control break programs

In this chapter, you learn how to read data from input files to keep you from interactively using the keyboard to enter large amounts of data. This is useful because most control break programs involve reading a large amount of data. You also learn how to write a single level control break program that accumulates totals. It is recommended that you do the exercises and labs in this chapter only after you have finished Chapter 7 of *Programming Logic and Design*.

FILE INPUT

When you write a business application, you usually have to use large amounts of data in the program. This data is stored in one or more files. As you learned in *Programming Logic and Design*, data is organized in a hierarchy. A field is part of this hierarchy. A **field** is a group of characters. A record is also part of the hierarchy. A **record** is a group of related fields. For example, in *Programming Logic and Design*, you studied a program that processes employee records. Each employee record consists of three fields: the employee's first name, the employee's last name, and the employee's department number.

In Java, to use the data stored in a file, you must first open the file and then read the data from the file into your program. You can use prewritten classes that are part of the Java 2 Platform to accomplish this. In subsequent sections, you learn how to import packages and classes to make the `BufferedReader` and `FileReader` classes available in your programs. You also learn how to use these classes to open a file and read data from a file.

IMPORTING PACKAGES AND CLASSES

A **package** is a group of related classes. The classes that you need in this chapter are part of a package named `java.io`. The Java 2 Platform contains many classes that are prewritten for you by the Java development team. You can simplify your programming tasks by creating objects using these classes. The objects will have attributes and methods that you can use in your Java programs.

To use these classes, you must import them into your Java programs. You use the `import` keyword to import a class from a Java package. The following code example imports the `BufferedReader` class from the Java package named `java.io`:

```
import java.io.BufferedReader;
```

You can use the * (asterisk) character in an import statement to import all classes from a package rather than specifying a single class. The following code example imports all of the classes in the `java.io` package. The programs in this chapter use this style to import the classes needed to perform file input.

```
import java.io.*;
```

TIP □ □ □ □ The `import` statement tells the Java compiler the name of the package and the name of the class(es) that contains the prewritten code you want to use. The Java compiler automatically includes this code.

OPENING A FILE

To open a file in Java, you instantiate a `FileReader` object and specify the name of the file to associate with the object. Look at the following example:

```
FileReader fr = new FileReader("inputFile.txt");
```

In the example, you use the `new` keyword to instantiate an object. A new `FileReader` object is instantiated that is associated with the file named `inputFile.txt`. Notice that the filename is enclosed in double quotation marks and placed within parentheses. As a result of the assignment statement, this newly created `FileReader` object is assigned to a variable named `fr` and you may now refer to it in your Java program using the name `fr`. In addition, the statement opens the file named `inputFile.txt` for reading, so you may now read data from the file.

Even though you can read from the file, it is usually better to read from a buffered file because it is more efficient. To do this, you must create a `BufferedReader` object by decorating the `FileReader` object. **Decorating** is a way to add functionality to objects in Java. Here is an example:

```
BufferedReader br = new BufferedReader(fr);
```

In this example, a new `BufferedReader` object is created by adding functionality to the `FileReader` object named `fr`. The name of the `BufferedReader` variable is `br`. You will use the name `br` to refer to the `BufferedReader` object in your Java program.

READING DATA FROM AN INPUT FILE

Once you have opened a file by creating a new `BufferedReader` object that decorates a `FileReader` object, you are ready to read the data in the file. The `BufferedReader` class provides this functionality with the `readLine()` method.

The `readLine()` method allows you to read a line from an input file. A **line** is defined as all of the characters up to a newline character or up to the End Of File (EOF) marker. The **newline** character is generated when you type the Enter key on the keyboard. The **EOF** marker is placed at the end of a file when it is saved.

In this chapter, we assume that the input file for a program is organized so that an employee's first name is on one line, followed by the last name on the next line, followed by a department number on the third line, as follows:

Tim

Moriarty

2

To read this data, you would write the following Java code.

```
String firstName, lastName, deptNum;
firstName = br.readLine();
lastName = br.readLine();
deptNum = br.readLine();
```

Because the `readLine()` method always returns a `String`, you declare three `String` variables named `firstName, lastName, and deptNum`. You then use the `readLine()` method three times to read the three lines of input from the file associated with the `BufferedReader` object named `br`. After this code executes, the variable named `firstName` contains the value "Tim", the variable named `lastName` contains the value "Moriarty", and the variable named `deptNum` contains the value "2".

READING DATA USING A LOOP AND EOF

When you read large amounts of data in a program, you usually want to continue to read from the file as part of a loop until you reach EOF. When using the `readLine()` method as part of a loop, you know when you reach EOF because the `readLine()` method returns a `null` value when EOF is reached. The Java code that follows illustrates using the `readLine()` method as part of a loop:

```
while((firstName = br.readLine()) != null)
{
    // Body of loop.
}
```

In this code sample, you include the `readLine()` method as part of the expression to be tested. As long as the value returned by `readLine()` is not equal to `null`, the expression is true and the loop is entered. As soon as EOF is encountered, the test is false and you will exit the loop. The parentheses are used to control precedence.

There is much more to learn about the input and output classes in the `java.io` package, but you can still accomplish quite a lot using only what you have learned in this section.

EXERCISE 5-1: OPENING FILES AND PERFORMING FILE INPUT

In this exercise, you use what you have learned about opening a file and getting input into a program from a file to study the following Java code. You then answer the subsequent questions about the code.

```
FileReader fr = new FileReader(myCarFile.dat);
BufferedReader br = new BufferedReader();
String carMake, carModel, modelYear;
carMake = br.readLine();
carModel = br.readLine();
modelYear = br.readLine();
```

1. There is an error on line 1. What must you do to fix it?

_____

2. There is also an error on line 2. What must you do to fix it?

_____

3. Consider the following data from the input file `myCarFile.dat`:

Honda Odyssey 2000

Cadillac Seville 2002

Ford Taurus 2003

a. What is the value stored in the variable named `carMake`?

_____

b. What is the value stored in the variable named `carModel`?

_____

c. What is the value stored in the variable named `modelYear`?

_____

d. If there is a problem with the values of these variables, state the problem and how you would fix it.

_____

LAB 5-1: USING AN INPUT FILE

In this lab, you open a file and read input from that file into a partially prewritten Java program. The program should read and print the names of animals that are stored in the input file named `animals.dat`.

1. Open the source code file named `Animals.java` using Notepad or the text editor of your choice.
2. Declare the variables you will need.
3. Write the Java statements that will open the input file, `animals.dat`, for reading.
4. Write a `while` loop to read the input until EOF is reached.
5. In the body of the loop, print the name of the animal.
6. Save this source code file in a directory of your choice, and then make that directory your working directory.
7. Compile the source code file `Animals.java`.
8. Execute the program.

ACCUMULATING TOTALS IN SINGLE-LEVEL CONTROL BREAK PROGRAMS

A **single-level control break** program causes a break in the logic based on the value of a single variable. The Bookstore program described in Chapter 7 of *Programming Logic and Design* is an example of this type of program. The Bookstore program reads a record for each book that a bookstore sells, keeps a count of the number of books in each category, and keeps a grand total of all of the books carried by the bookstore. The report generated by this program includes book titles, a count of the number of books in each category, and a count of all books. Each book record is made up of the following fields: Book Title and Book Category. Note the following example records, each comprising two lines:

> The Road Less Traveled
>
> Self Help
>
> Family Medical Guide
>
> Reference

Note that you can look at this program written in Java by opening the file named `Totals.java`. Note also that the program in this section contains slightly different logic than that presented in *Programming Logic and Design*. All of the code is included in the `main()` method rather than writing separate methods to implement the modules discussed.

Figure 5-1 includes the mainline pseudocode developed in *Programming Logic and Design* for this program, as well as the Java code needed to implement this part of the program.

FIGURE 5-1: BOOKSTORE PROGRAM—`mainline()` MODULE

```
start
        perform startUp()
        while not eof
            perform bookListLoop()
        endwhile
        perform closeDown()
stop


// Totals.java - This program creates a report that lists
// all of the books carried by a bookstore with a count
// for each book category and a grand total.
// Input:  books.dat.
// Output: Report.

import java.io.*;  // Import class for file input.

public class Totals
{
    public static void main(String args[]) throws Exception
    {
        // Perform startUp() module work here.
        while(bookTitle != null)   // Check for EOF.
        {
            // Perform bookListLoop() module work here.
        }
        // Perform closeDown() module work here.
    } // End of main() method.

} // End of Totals class.
```

As you can see, the Java program begins with comments that describe what the program does as well as the name of the input file and the program's output. Next, you see an `import` statement that tells the compiler to include the classes that are part of the `java.io` package. Then you define the `Totals` class, and within the class, you write the `main()` method.

You know how to write a header for the `main()` method. Now you must include the words `throws Exception` as part of the header. These must be included because opening a file and using the `readLine()` method in this program could cause an exception to occur as your program executes. (An **exception** is an event that disrupts the normal flow of execution.) In this program, the event could try to open a nonexistent file or try to read beyond the EOF marker. You must include `throws Exception` or this program will not compile. By doing so, you tell the Java compiler that you know an exception could occur; the compiler trusts that you will handle the problem should it occur.

TIP □ □ □ □ | There is much to learn in order to do proper exception handling in Java programs. For now, however, this is how we will handle this type of exception.

Within the `main()` method you perform the work of the `startUp()` module and then set up your loop that checks for the end of file. Within the loop you perform the work of the `bookListLoop()` module. When you exit the EOF loop, you perform the work of the `closeDown()` module. To begin, look at the work defined in the `startUp()` module. Figure 5-2 includes the pseudocode and the corresponding Java code for the `startUp()` module.

As shown in Figure 5-2, you first declare variables. Next, you open the input file `books.dat` by instantiating a `FileReader` object and decorating it with the functionality of a `BufferedReader` object. You then print two blank lines followed by the heading of the report.

Now you are ready to perform a priming read to get the first input record. You learned about performing a priming read in Chapter 4 of this book and in Chapter 2 of *Programming Logic and Design*. As you learned in a previous section of this chapter, you will read the fields of the record one at a time using the `readLine()` method. However, this introduces a problem. The first field in the book record is the book's title followed by the book's category. With these facts about the record in mind, assume a situation in which you try to read a book title, but instead of reading a title, you encounter the EOF marker. If you then continue to try to read the book's category, your program will cause an exception to occur because you are attempting to read beyond the EOF marker. To avoid this, you must place the first `readLine()` that reads the book's title in an `if` statement that checks for EOF. If EOF is not encountered, then the statement in the `if` statement executes to read the book's category.

After you read in the first record, you assign the value of the current record's book category, `bookCategory`, to the variable named `previousCategory`. You use the variable `bookCategory` as your control break variable.

FIGURE 5-2: BOOKSTORE PROGRAM—**startUp()** MODULE

```
startUp()
      declare variables
      open files
      print heading
      read bookRecord
      previousCategory = bookCategory
return


String head1 = "BOOK LIST";
String bookTitle = "";         // Current record book title.
String bookCategory = "";      // Current record book category.
String previousCategory = ""; // Previous record book category.
double grandTotal = 0;         // Count of all books.
double categoryTotal = 0;      // Count of books in a category.

// Open input file.
FileReader fr = new FileReader("books.dat");
// Create BufferedReader object.
BufferedReader br = new BufferedReader(fr);

// Print two blank lines.
System.out.println();
System.out.println();
// Print heading.
System.out.println(head1);
// Read first record from file.
if((bookTitle = br.readLine()) != null) // Test for EOF.
{
      bookCategory = br.readLine();
}
previousCategory = bookCategory;
```

Now that the **startUp()** work is done, you can look at the logic and Java code for the work done in the **bookListLoop()**. Figure 5-3 includes this pseudocode and Java code.

As you can see in Figure 5-3, within the body of the EOF loop, you use the **compareTo()** method to test the control break variable **bookCategory**. You want to know if the record with which you are currently working has the same category as the previous record's category. If it does not, you know that you are beginning a new category and you perform the work of the **categoryChange()** module, which is the control break module. This includes the following:

1. Print the value of **categoryTotal**, which contains the count of books in the current category.
2. Add the value of **categoryTotal** to **grandTotal**, which is the variable used to accumulate the total of all books.

3. Assign 0 to the variable named `categoryTotal` to get ready to keep a count of the books in the next category.

4. Save the value of the current category, `bookCategory`, as the previous category, `previousCategory`.

FIGURE 5-3: BOOKSTORE PROGRAM—**bookListLoop( )** MODULE

```
bookListLoop()
    if bookCategory not equal to previousCategory
        perform categoryChange()
    endif
    print bookTitle
    categoryTotal = categoryTotal + 1
    read bookRec
return

categoryChange()
    print "Category count", categoryTotal
    grandTotal = grandTotal + categoryTotal
    categoryTotal = 0
    previousCategory = bookCategory
return



while(bookTitle != null)    // check for EOF
{
    // Check control break variable.
    if(bookCategory.compareTo(previousCategory) != 0)
    {
        // This is the categoryChange() module work.
        System.out.println(previousCategory +
                "Category Count:  " + categoryTotal);
        System.out.println();
        System.out.println();
        grandTotal += categoryTotal;
        categoryTotal = 0;
        previousCategory = bookCategory;
    }
    System.out.println(bookTitle);
    categoryTotal++;
    // Read next record and test for EOF.
    if((bookTitle = br.readLine()) != null)
        bookCategory = br.readLine();
}
```

Following the `categoryChange( )` work, the next statement prints the book's title either after a category has changed or as part of the current category. You then add 1 to the category counter variable named `categoryTotal`. Finally, you read the next book record from the input file using the same technique described as part of the `startUp( )` module work. As you saw in Figure 5-1, the last section of this program is the work done in the `closeDown( )` module. Figure 5-4 includes this pseudocode and Java code.

FIGURE 5-4: BOOKSTORE PROGRAM—`closeDown()` MODULE

```
closeDown()
     perform categoryChange()
     print "Total number of book titles", grandTotal
     close files
return



// This is the categoryChange() module work.
System.out.println(previousCategory + " Category Count:   " +
                   categoryTotal);
System.out.println();
System.out.println();
grandTotal += categoryTotal;
categoryTotal = 0;
previousCategory = bookCategory;
System.out.println("Total number of book titles: " +
                   grandTotal);
br.close();
System.exit(0);
```

As you can see in Figure 5-4, the work includes performing the work done in the `categoryChange()` module again. Remember that the `categoryChange()` module is the control break module. Then you print the value of `grandTotal`, which now contains the total of all books carried by the bookstore. Finally, you close the input file and exit the program. You close the input file by using the `BufferedReader` object, `br`, to invoke the `close()` method.

EXERCISE 5-2: ACCUMULATING TOTALS IN SINGLE-LEVEL CONTROL BREAK PROGRAMS

In this exercise, you use what you have learned about accumulating totals in a single-level control break program to answer specific questions. First, study the Java code that follows:

```
if(price != oldPrice)
{
    System.out.println("Price Group " + oldPrice);
    grandTotal = price;
    oldPrice = price;
}
```

1. What is the control break variable?

2. The value of the control break variable should never be changed. True or False?

3. Is the `grandTotal` being calculated correctly?

    _____

    If not, how can you fix the code?

    _____

4. In a control break program, it doesn't matter if the records in the input file are in a specified order. True or False?

    _____

LAB 5-2: ACCUMULATING TOTALS IN SINGLE-LEVEL CONTROL BREAK PROGRAMS

In this lab, you use what you have learned about accumulating totals in a single-level control break program to complete a partially prewritten Java program. The program is described in Chapter 7, Exercise 3 in *Programming Logic and Design*. The program should produce a report that prints each sales transaction detail, with a total at the end of each department and the total sales for all departments. Read the problem description carefully and look over the input file, `department.dat`, before you begin.

In the program, note that variables have been declared and the `housekeeping()` work has been done for you. You need to implement the control break portion of the program, which is the work done when a new record is read that has a different department number. Be sure to accumulate the department totals and the grand total for all departments. You must also implement the work done in the `cleanUp()` module. There are comments in the code that tell you where to write your statements. You can use the Bookstore program in this chapter as a guide.

1. Open the source code file named `Department.java` using Notepad or the text editor of your choice.
2. Study the prewritten code to understand what has already been done.
3. Write an `if` statement in the body of the `while` loop to test the control break variable.
4. Write the control break code.
5. Print the transaction number and transaction amount.
6. Add the transaction amount to the department total.
7. Read the next record.
8. Do the `cleanUp()` work that includes printing the department number and department total, adding the last department total to the grand total, and printing the total sales.
9. Save this source code file in a directory of your choice and then make that directory your working directory.
10. Compile the source code file, `Department.java`.
11. Execute the program.

6

USING ARRAYS IN JAVA PROGRAMS

After studying Chapter 6, you will be able to:

☐ Use arrays in Java programs

☐ Search an array for a particular value

☐ Use parallel arrays in a Java program

In this chapter, you learn how to use Java to declare and initialize arrays. You then access the elements of an array to assign values and process them within your program. You also learn why it is important to stay within the bounds of an array. In addition, you study some programs written in Java that implement the logic and design presented in your *Programming Logic and Design* book.

It is recommended that you do the exercises and labs in this chapter only after you have finished Chapter 8 of *Programming Logic and Design*.

ARRAY BASICS

An **array** is a group of data items in which every item has the same data type, is referenced using the same variable name, and is stored consecutively in memory. To reference individual elements in an array, you use a subscript. A **subscript** is an integer that is used to calculate an offset into the array. Think of a subscript as the position number of a value within an array. It is important for you to know that in Java, subscript values begin with 0 (zero) and end with n-1, where n is the number of items stored in the array.

Before you look at Java programs that use arrays, you must first learn how to declare an array, possibly initialize an array with predetermined values, access array elements, and stay within the bounds of an array.

DECLARING ARRAYS

Before you can use an array in a Java program, you must first declare it. An example of how to declare an array of data type `int` and another array of data type `String` follows:

```
int zipCodes[] = new int[10];
String cities[] = new String[4];
```

As shown, you begin by specifying the data type of the items that will be stored in the array. The data type is followed by the name of the array and then a pair of square brackets.

TIP □ □ □ □ It is an error to place anything within the pair of square brackets that follows the array name; the integer belongs in the second pair of brackets.

The `new` operator is then used to allocate enough memory for the array elements, based on the data type specified and the integer value placed within the second pair of square brackets that follows the data type. As shown in Figure 6-1, the compiler allocates enough consecutive memory locations to store 10 elements of data type `int` for the array named `zipCodes`. If `zipCodes[0]` is stored at memory address 1000, then the address of `zipCodes[9]` is 1036 because each `int` requires 4 bytes of memory.

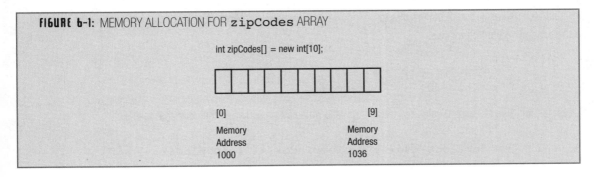

FIGURE 6-1: MEMORY ALLOCATION FOR `zipCodes` ARRAY

The `zipCodes` array provides an example of how arrays that contain primitive data types are allocated. Memory allocation is different for arrays of objects. Because a `String` is an object in Java, not a primitive data type, memory is allocated for references to a `String` object rather than the `String` object itself. A **reference** is the memory address of an object. The memory for the `String` object is allocated when the `String` object is created. This is shown in Figure 6-2.

FIGURE 6-2: MEMORY ALLOCATION FOR `cities` ARRAY

As shown in Figure 6-2, the compiler allocates enough consecutive memory locations to store 4 references to `String` objects for the array named `cities`. If the address of `cities[0]` is 1000, then the address of `cities[3]` is 1012 because each reference requires 4 bytes of memory. When a `String` object is created, the compiler allocates memory for it at another memory address. This address is then stored in the array. If the first `String` object created stores the name of the city, Chicago, and the memory allocated for Chicago begins at address 1200, then address 1200 is stored in the first element of the array. An example of creating `String` objects is presented later in this chapter.

INITIALIZING ARRAYS

In Java, array elements are automatically initialized to 0 (zero) for numeric data types and to the value null for references. **Null** is a special value in Java that is the zero value for references.

You can and will sometimes want to initialize arrays with values that you choose. This can be done when you declare the array. To initialize an array when you declare it, use curly braces to surround a comma-delimited list of data items, as shown in the example code that follows:

```
int zipCodes[] = {60616, 48324, 60510};
String cities[] = {"Chicago", "Detroit", "Batavia"};
```

You can also use assignment statements to provide values for array elements after an array is declared. This is shown in the example code that follows:

```
zipCodes[0] = 60616;
cities[0] = "Chicago";
```

A loop is often used to assign values to the elements in an array, as shown in the code that follows:

```
for(loopIndex = 0; loopIndex < 3; loopIndex++)
{
  zipCodes[loopIndex] = 12345;
  cities[loopIndex] = "AnyCity";
}
```

The first time this loop is encountered, `loopIndex` is assigned the value `0`. Because `0` is less than `3`, the body of the loop executes, assigning the value `12345` to `zipCodes[0]` and the value `"AnyCity"` to `cities[0]`. The second time the loop executes, the value of `loopIndex` has been incremented and the value `12345` is now assigned to `zipCodes[1]` and `"AnyCity"` is assigned to `cities[1]`. Each time the loop executes, the value of `loopIndex` is incremented. This allows you to access a different location in the arrays each time the body of the loop executes.

ACCESSING ARRAY ELEMENTS

You need to access individual locations in an array when you assign a value to an array element, print its value, change its value, assign the value to another variable, and so forth. In Java, you use an integer expression placed in square brackets to indicate which array element should be accessed. This integer expression is the subscript.

TIP ▫ ▫ ▫ ▫ | Remember that subscript values begin with 0 (zero) in Java.

The Java program that follows this paragraph declares an array of data type `double`, initializes an array of data type `double`, copies values from one array to another, changes several values stored in the array named `target`, and prints the values of the arrays named `source` and `target`. You can compile and execute this program if you like. It is stored in the file named `ArrayTest.java`.

```
public class ArrayTest
{
   public static void main(String args[])
   {
      double target[] = new double[3];
      double source[] = {1.0, 5.5, 7.9};
      int loopIndex;
      // Copy values from source to target.
      for(loopIndex = 0; loopIndex < 3; loopIndex++)
         target[loopIndex] = source[loopIndex];
```

```
        // Assign values to two elements of target.
        target[0] = 2.0;
        target[1] = 4.5;
        // Print values stored in source and target.
        for(loopIndex = 0; loopIndex < 3; loopIndex++)
        {
            System.out.println("Source " + source[loopIndex]);
            System.out.println("Target " + target[loopIndex]);
        }
    }
}
```

STAYING WITHIN THE BOUNDS OF AN ARRAY

As a Java programmer, you must be careful to ensure that the subscript values you use to access array elements are within the legal bounds. The Java interpreter checks to make sure that a subscript used in your program is greater than or equal to 0 and less than the length of the array. For example, if you declare an array named `numbers` as `int numbers[] = new int[10];` Java checks to be sure the subscripts you use to access this array are integer values between 0 and 9.

TIP ▫ ▫ ▫ ▫ | When using a loop to access the elements in an array, be sure that the test you use to terminate the loop keeps you within the legal bounds, 0 to *n*-1, where *n* is the number of items stored in the array.

If you access an array element that is not in the legal bounds, Java generates an `ArrayIndexOutOfBounds Exception`. As you have learned, an exception indicates an error in your program and can cause your program to terminate.

EXERCISE 6-1: WORKING WITH ARRAY BASICS

In this exercise, you use what you have learned about declaring and initializing arrays to begin working with array basics.

1. Write array declarations for each of the following:

    a. five ages _____

    b. three names _____

    c. ten salaries _____

2. Declare and initialize arrays that store the following:

    a. The ages 15, 54, 23, 3, and 22 _____

    b. The names Johnson, Egan, and Benson _____

    c. The salaries 25,000.00, 35,000.00, and 45,000.00 _____

3. Write an assignment statement that assigns the value 96 to the first element of the array of integers named `tests`. _____

LAB 6-1: USING ARRAYS

In this lab, you complete a partially prewritten Java program that uses arrays. The program is described in Chapter 8, Exercise 1, in *Programming Logic and Design*. The program should produce a count of the number of citizens residing in each of 22 voting districts.

Read the problem description carefully and look over the input file, `census.dat`, before you begin. Variables have been declared, and the loop and the output statement have been written. You need to open the input file, read the first record, and write the code within the EOF `while` loop that uses the array to accumulate totals. There are comments in the code that tell you where to write your statements.

1. Open the source code file named `Census.java` using Notepad or the text editor of your choice.
2. Write the Java statements that will open the input file, `census.dat`, for reading.
3. Read the first record from the input file.
4. In the body of the loop, write the code that will accumulate a count of citizens by district in the array and then read the next record.
5. Save this source code file in a directory of your choice and then make that directory your working directory.
6. Compile the source code file, `Census.java`.
7. Execute the program.

SEARCHING AN ARRAY FOR AN EXACT MATCH

One of the programs described in *Programming Logic and Design* uses an array to hold valid item numbers for a mail-order business. When a customer orders an item, you want to determine if the customer ordered a valid item number by searching through the array for that item number. This program uses a technique called setting a flag to verify that an item exists in an array. The pseudocode and the Java code for this program are shown in Figure 6-3.

As shown in Figure 6-3, when you translate the pseudocode to Java, you make a few changes. You assign the value `false` instead of the string constant `"N"` to the variable named `foundIt`, which is used as the flag. This is because Java has a primitive data type that may be used to store `true` and `false` values. This data type is the `boolean` data type. Also, instead of assigning the value `1` to the variable named `x` before the loop is entered, you assign the value `0` to `x` in the first expression of the `for` loop. You assign `0` instead of `1` to `x` because, as you have learned, the first element in a Java array is numbered 0. Also, rather than adding `1` to `x` after the `if` statement, you increment `x` in the third expression of the `for` loop.

FIGURE 6-3: PSEUDOCODE AND JAVA CODE FOR THE MAIL-ORDER PROGRAM

```
x = 1
foundIt = "N"
while x < 7
    if custItemNo = validItem[x] then
        foundIt = "Y"
    endif
    x = x + 1
endwhile
if foundIt = "N" then
    print "No such item"
endif


boolean foundIt;
foundIt = false; // Start out with flag set to false.
// Search for item number.
for(x = 0; x < 6; x++)
{
   if(custItemNo == validItem[x])
      foundIt = true;       // Set flag to true.
}
// Test flag to see if item was found.
if(foundIt == false)
   System.out.println("No such item.");
```

TIP ☐ ☐ ☐ ☐ Notice that the equality operator, ==, is used when comparing the `int` value in the first `if` statement and the `boolean` value in the second `if` statement.

The entire program can be found in the file named `MailOrder.java`. You may want to compile and execute the program to see how it operates.

EXERCISE 6-2: SEARCHING AN ARRAY FOR AN EXACT MATCH

In this exercise, you use what you have learned about searching an array for an exact match to study the Java code that follows, and then you answer some questions.

First, study the Java code that follows:

```
String cities[] = {"Chicago", "Gary", "Tampa", "Boston"};
int foundIt, i;
String inCity;
inCity = JOptionPane.showInputDialog("Enter city name: ");
for(i = 0, i <= 4; i++)
{
  if(inCity == cities[i])
  {
    foundIt = true;
  }
}
```

1. Is the `for` loop written correctly?

   _____

   If not, what should you do to fix it?

   _____

2. Which variable is the flag?

   _____

3. Is the flag variable declared correctly?

   _____

   If not, what should you do to fix it?

   _____

4. Is the comparison in the `if` statement done correctly?

   _____

   If not, what should you do to fix it?

   _____

LAB 6-2: SEARCHING AN ARRAY FOR AN EXACT MATCH

In this lab, you use what you have learned about searching an array to find an exact match to complete a partially prewritten Java program. The program uses an array that contains valid zip codes for 20 suburbs of Chicago. You ask the user of the program to enter a zip code, and your program then searches the array for that zip code. If it is not found, print a message that informs the user that the zip code is not found in your list of valid zip codes.

Variables have been declared and input statements are written. You need to use a loop to examine all the items in the array and test for a match. You also need to set a flag if there is a match, and then test the flag variable to determine if you should print the "Zip code not found." message. There are comments in the code that tell you where to write your statements. You can use the Mail Order program in this chapter as a guide.

1. Open the source code file named `ZipCodes.java` using Notepad or the text editor of your choice.
2. Study the prewritten code to understand what has already been done.
3. Write a loop statement that allows you to examine the zip codes stored in the array.
4. Test to see if there is a match.
5. If there is not a match, print the message "Zip code not found."
6. Save this source code file in a directory of your choice, and then make that directory your working directory.
7. Compile the source code file, `ZipCodes.java`.
8. Execute the program using the following as input:
   60515
   61111
   62417
   12345

PARALLEL ARRAYS

As you have learned in *Programming Logic and Design*, you use parallel arrays to store values to maintain a relationship between the items. Figure 6-4 shows that the student ID number stored in `stuID[0]` and the grade stored in `grades[0]` are related—student 56 received a grade of 99.

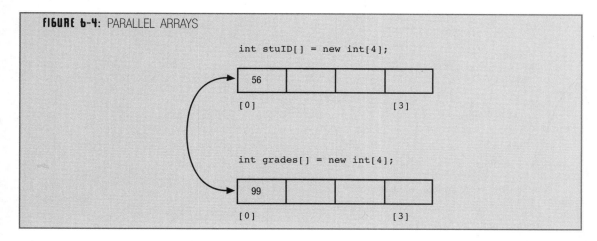

FIGURE 6-4: PARALLEL ARRAYS

```
int stuID[] = new int[4];
```

| 56 | | | |

[0]   [3]

```
int grades[] = new int[4];
```

| 99 | | | |

[0]   [3]

This relationship is established by using the same subscript value when accessing each array. Note that the programmer must maintain this relationship. Java does not create or maintain the relationship.

One of the programs discussed in *Programming Logic and Design* is an expanded version of the mail-order program discussed in the "Searching an Array for an Exact Match" section of the chapter you are now reading. In this expanded program, you want to determine the price of the ordered item, multiply that price by the quantity ordered, and print a bill. You use parallel arrays to help you organize the data for the program. One array, `validItem`, contains six valid item numbers. The other array, `validItemPrice`, contains six valid prices. Each price is in the same position as the corresponding item number in the other array. When a customer orders an item, you search the `validItem` array for the customer's item number. When the item number is found, you use the price stored in the same location of the `validItemPrice` array to calculate the customer's bill. The complete Java program is stored in the file named `MailOrder2.java`. The pseudocode and Java code that search the `validItem` array and use a price from the `validItemPrice` array to calculate the customer's bill are shown in Figure 6-5.

FIGURE 6-5: PSEUDOCODE AND JAVA CODE FOR **MailOrder2** PROGRAM

```
foundIt = "No"
x = 1
while x <= 6
        if(custItemNo = validItem[x] then
                totBill = validItemPrice[x] * custQuantity
                print custName, totBill
                foundIt = "Yes"
                x = x + 1
        else
                x = x + 1
        endif
endwhile
if foundIt not equal to "Yes" then
        print "Error"
endif


foundIt = false;
x = 0;
// Search for item number within bounds of the array.
while(x < 6)
{
   if(custItemNo == validItem[x])
   {
      totBill = validItemPrice[x] * custQuantity;
      System.out.println(custName + " $" + totBill);
      foundIt = true;
      x++;
   }
   else
      x++;
}
if(foundIt != true)
   System.out.println("Error: Invalid Item Number.");
```

EXERCISE 6-3: USING PARALLEL ARRAYS

In this exercise, you use what you have learned about using parallel arrays in a program to study code, and then you answer some questions.

First, study the Java code that follows:

```
String cities[] = "Berwyn", "Aurora", "Lisle", "Palatine";
int zipCodes[] = 60402, 60504, 60532, 60038;
boolean saveIt;
int i, x;
String inCity;
inCity = JOptionPane.showInputDialog("Enter city name: ");
for(i = 0; i = 4; ++i)
{
```

```
    if(inCity.compareTo(cities[i]) == 0)
    {
      saveIt = i;
    }
  }
  System.out.println("Zip code for " + cities[saveIt] +
                          " is " + zipCodes[saveIt]);
```

1. Are the arrays declared and initialized correctly?

   _____

   If not, what should you do to fix them?

   _____

2. Is the `for` loop written correctly?

   _____

   If not, what should you do to fix it?

   _____

3. As written, how many times will the `for` loop execute?

   _____

4. How would you describe the purpose of the statement `saveIt = i;`?

   _____

LAB 6-3: USING PARALLEL ARRAYS

In this lab, you use what you have learned about parallel arrays to complete a partially prewritten Java program. The program is described in Chapter 8, Exercise 7 in *Programming Logic and Design*. The program should print a price for a fast-food item or the message "Sorry, we do not carry that." as output.

Read the problem description carefully before you begin. Variables have been declared and initialized, if necessary, and the input has been done for you. You need to write the rest of the program that searches for the name of the food item and either prints its price or the error message if the item is not found. There are comments in the code that tell you where to write your statements. You can use the expanded Mail Order program in this chapter as a guide.

1. Open the source code file named `FastFood.java` using Notepad or the text editor of your choice.
2. Study the prewritten code to understand what has already been done.
3. Write the code that searches the array for the name of the food item ordered by the customer.
4. Print the price of the food item or the message.
5. Save this source code file in a directory of your choice, and then make that directory your working directory.

6. Compile the source code file, `FastFood.java`.

7. Execute the program using the following data:

```
12345      Cheeseburger
54321      Coke
98765      Chips
56789      Fries
33333      Pepsi
10001      Hamburger
```

8. Record the output:

_____

_____

SORTING DATA AND ADVANCED ARRAY MANIPULATION

After studying Chapter 7, you will be able to:

- ☐ Understand why data needs to be sorted
- ☐ Swap two values in a program
- ☐ Use a bubble sort to order data in a Java program
- ☐ Use multidimensional arrays to organize data in a Java program

In this chapter, you review why you may want to sort data, how to use Java to swap two data values in a program, and how a Java program uses a bubble sort. You also learn about using multidimensional arrays in Java. It is recommended that you do the exercises and labs in this chapter only after you have finished Chapter 9 of your book, *Programming Logic and Design*.

TIP □ □ □ □ | Chapter 7 of this book corresponds to Chapter 9 in *Programming Logic and Design, Third Edition, Comprehensive*. If you are using *Programming Logic and Design, Third Edition, Introductory*, you have only Chapters 1–8. Nonetheless, the chapter you are about to read is provided as a bridge to further study. If necessary, your instructor can give you the corresponding chapter from the *Logic Comprehensive* book.

WHY SHOULD DATA BE SORTED?

Data records are always stored in some order, but possibly not in the order in which you want to process or view them in your program. When this is the case, you need to sort the records so that they are in a useful order. For example, the records you need to process might be stored in product-number order, but you need to produce a report listing products from lowest to highest cost. For your program, you need to sort the records by cost.

Sorting also makes searching for records easier and more efficient. When you need to search for a record that contains a particular data value, if the records are not in some order, you must examine every record to find it or find out that it does not exist. However, when the records are in order, you know when to stop searching, as shown in the following step-by-step scenario:

1. The records used by your program are sorted by product number.
2. You are searching for product number 12367.
3. You reach the record for product number 12368 and have not yet found product number 12367.
4. At this point, you would know that the record for product number 12367 does not exist and you can stop searching through the list.

Many search algorithms that you can use when designing a program require that data be in sorted order before the data can be searched. (An **algorithm** is a plan for solving a problem.) There are many search algorithms and also algorithms for sorting data. In *Programming Logic and Design*, you learned about the bubble sort, insertion sort, and selection sort, which are examples of sort algorithms. The binary search is an example of a search algorithm, but this algorithm is not covered in this book.

SWAPPING DATA VALUES

When you swap values, you place the value stored in one variable into a second variable, and then you place the value in the second variable into the first variable. You must also create a third variable to temporarily hold one of the values you want to swap, so that a value is not lost. For example, if you try to swap values using the following code, you lose the value of `score2`:

```
int score1 = 90;
int score2 = 85;
score2 = score1;    // The value of score2 is 90.
score1 = score2;    // The value of score1 is also 90.
```

However, if you use a variable to temporarily hold one of the values, the swap is successful. This is shown in the following code:

```
int score1 = 90;
int score2 = 85;
int temp;
temp = score2;      // The value of temp is 85.
score2 = score1;    // The value of score2 is 90.
score1 = temp;      // The value of score1 is 85.
```

EXERCISE 7-1: SWAPPING VALUES

In this exercise, you use what you have learned about swapping values to complete the following related task:

1. You have declared and initialized two `String` variables, `product1` and `product2`, in a Java program. Now, you want to swap the values stored in `product1` and `product2` but only if the value of `product1` is greater than the value of `product2`. Remember that you do not use the equality operator (`==`) when comparing `String` objects. Write the Java code that accomplishes this task. The declarations are as follows:

```
String product1 = "desk";
String product2 = "chair";
```

_____

_____

_____

_____

LAB 7-1: SWAPPING VALUES

In this lab, you complete a partially prewritten Java program that swaps values stored in three `int` variables and determines maximum and minimum values. Variables have been declared and the input and output statements have been written. You need to write the statements that compare the values and swap them if appropriate. There are comments in the code that tell you where to write your statements.

1. Open the source code file named `MinMax.java` using Notepad or the text editor of your choice.
2. Write the statements that test the first two numbers and swap them if necessary.

3. Write the statements that test the second and third numbers and swap them if necessary.

4. Write the statements that test the first and second numbers again and swap them if necessary.

5. Save this source code file in a directory of your choice, and then make that directory your working directory.

6. Compile the source code file, `MinMax.java`.

7. Execute the program using the following sets of input values and record the output:

30	26	3
10	30	20
23	45	23

_____

_____

_____

_____

USING A BUBBLE SORT

A bubble sort is one of the simplest sorting techniques to understand. However, while it is logically simple, it is not very efficient. If the list contains *n* values, the bubble sort will make *n* - 1 passes over the list. For example, if the list contains 100 values, the bubble sort will make 99 passes over the data. During each pass, it examines successive overlapped pairs and swaps or exchanges those values that are out of order. After one pass over the data, the heaviest (largest) value sinks to the bottom and is in the correct position in the list.

In *Programming Logic and Design*, you learned several ways to refine the bubble sort. One refinement is to reduce unnecessary comparisons. You can do this because on the second pass over the data when using a bubble sort, you know that you can ignore the last value in the list because it is in its proper position. On the third pass, you do not have to worry about the last two values in the list because they are already positioned correctly. Thus, in each pass, you can reduce the number of items to be compared, and possibly swapped, by one.

Another refinement to the bubble sort is to eliminate unnecessary passes over the data in the list. When items in the array to be sorted are not entirely out of order, it may not be necessary to make *n* - 1 passes over the data because after several passes, they may already be in order. By adding a flag variable to the bubble sort, you can use the flag to test whether any swaps have been made in any single pass over the data. If no swaps have been made, you know that the list is in order, and therefore you do not need to continue with additional passes.

You also learned about using a variable for the size of the array to make your logic easier to understand and your programs easier to change and maintain. Another refinement you learned about is how to sort a list of variable size by counting the number of items placed in the array as you read in those items from an input file.

All of these refinements are included in the Java program in Figure 7-1.

FIGURE 7-1: MAINLINE LOGIC FOR SCORE SORTING PROGRAM

```
start
        perform housekeeping()
        perform sortScores()
        perform finishUp()
stop
```

THE HOUSEKEEPING() MODULE

The work done in the `housekeeping()` module includes declaring variables, opening the input file, reading in the data from the input file, and storing the data in an array. It also includes counting the number of elements stored in the array and checking to be sure there is room in the array for all the data items.

Figure 7-2 includes the pseudocode and the Java code that implements the work done in the `housekeeping()` module.

FIGURE 7-2: WORK DONE IN `housekeeping()` MODULE

```
housekeeping()
     declare variables
     open files
     read inScore
     while not eof
           if x > 100 then
                   print "Warning! Too many scores."
                   extraEls = extraEls + 1
           else
                   score[x] = inScore
           endif
           x = x + 1
           read inScore
     endwhile
     numberOfEls = x - extraEls
     if extraEls > 0 then
           print "Warning. ", extraEls, " elements from the input file
                   will not be included in the sort."
     endif
return


// This is the work of the housekeeping() module.
// Declare variables.
int inScore = 0;                // Student score.
String scoreString;             // String version of score.
int score[] = new int[100];     // Array of student scores.
int x = 0;                      // Array subscript.
int numberOfEls;                // Actual number of elements in array.
int extraEls = 0;               // Number of elements that don't fit.
int temp;                       // Used to swap values.
boolean switchOccurred;         // Flag.
int pairsToCompare;             // Number of pairs in list to compare.

// Open input file.
FileReader fr = new FileReader("scores.dat");
// Create BufferedReader object.
```

FIGURE 7-2: WORK DONE IN `housekeeping()` MODULE (CONTINUED)

```
BufferedReader br = new BufferedReader(fr);

// Read first record from file.
if((scoreString = br.readLine()) != null) // Test for EOF.
      // Convert String to integer.
      inScore = Integer.parseInt(scoreString);

while(scoreString != null)    // Check for EOF.
{
      // Test for values that cannot be put in array.
      if(x > 99)
      {
            System.out.println("Warning! Too many scores.");
            // Increment number of elements that cannot fit in array.
            extraEls++;
      }
      else
            // Place value in array.
            score[x] = inScore;

      x++;    // Get ready for next input item.

      // Read next score.
      if((scoreString = br.readLine()) != null) // Test for EOF.
            // Convert String to integer.
            inScore = Integer.parseInt(scoreString);
}  // End of EOF loop.

// Calculate number of items to sort.
numberOfEls = x - extraEls;

// Tell user how many items would not fit in array.
if(extraEls > 0)
      System.out.println("Warning. " + extraEls +
      " elements from the input file will not be sorted.");
```

As you can see in the Java code shown in Figure 7-2, variables are declared first. Notice that the variable named `switchOccurred` is declared as data type `boolean`. Also notice that the array subscript variable, `x`, is initialized to 0 because the first position in an array is position 0.

Next you open the input file and create the `BufferedReader` object, `br`. Once the input file is open, you read in the first student score and convert the `String` returned by the `readLine()` method to an `int` using the `parseInt()` method. Next, you test for EOF as part of the `while` loop. As long as you are not done reading the input file, you use the `if` statement, `if(x > 99)`, to test to make sure you have enough room in the array to store the student score. If not, you warn your user and then add one to `extraEls`, which is the name of the variable used to count the number of elements that do not fit in the array.

If there is room in the array, you assign the student score, `inScore`, to the array named `score` using the value of `x` as a subscript to specify the position in the array. You then increment the value of `x` to get ready to store the next student score in the array. In the last statement of the loop, you read in the next student score and repeat the statements in the loop until you have read in all the scores from the input file.

When you exit the loop, you can calculate the number of items stored in the array by subtracting the number of extra elements, `extraEls`, from the value of `x`. You can use the value of `x` in this calculation because you incremented it every time the loop executed. The number of times the loop executed represents the number of student scores you read from the input file.

Using another `if` statement, you now check to see if any student scores were not placed in the array. If so, you tell your user how many items were not included in the array and therefore will not be sorted.

THE SORTSCORES() AND SWITCHVALUES() MODULES

In the `sortScores()` module, you use a refined bubble sort to rearrange the student scores in the array named `score` to be in ascending order. Figure 7-3 includes the pseudocode and the Java code that implements the work done in the `sortScores()` module and the `switchValues()` module.

As you can see in Figure 7-3, you begin by calculating the number of pairs you will compare (`pairsToCompare`) in the first pass of the bubble sort by subtracting one from the number of elements in the array, `numberOfEls`. You do this because you do not want to compare item `x` in the array with item `x+1` when `x` is the last item in the array. You then set the flag variable, `switchOccurred`, to `true` because you assume the data items are out of order and some or all of the items will need to be swapped.

The outer loop, `while(switchOccurred == true)`, controls the number of passes you will make over the data in the array. You use this logic to implement one of the refinements discussed earlier—to eliminate unnecessary passes over the data. As long as `switchOccurred` is true, you will enter the loop because you know that swaps were made and this means the data is still out of order. The first statement in the body of the loop is `x = 0;`. This differs from the statement in the pseudocode because you are using `x` as the array subscript, and, in Java, the first subscript in an array is number 0.

Next, to prepare for comparing the elements in the array, you assign the value `false` to `switchOccurred`. You do this because you have not yet swapped any values in the array on this pass. The inner loop, `while(x < pairsToCompare)`, controls the number of pairs of values in the array you will compare on this pass over the data. This implements another of the refinements discussed earlier—to reduce unnecessary comparisons. The last statement in the outer loop, `pairsToCompare--;`, decrements the value of `pairsToCompare` by one each time the outer loop executes. You do this because when a complete pass is made over the data, you know that an item was positioned in the array correctly. Comparing the value of `pairsToCompare` with the value of `x` in the inner loop allows you to reduce the number of comparisons made when this loop executes.

FIGURE 7-3: WORK DONE IN THE `sortScores()` AND `switchValues()` MODULES

```
sortScores()
     pairsToCompare = numberOfEls -1
     switchOccurred = "Yes"
     while switchOccurred = "Yes"
          x = 1
          switchOccurred = "No"
          while x <= pairsToCompare
               if score[x] > score[x+1] then
                    perform switchValues()
                    switchOccurred = "Yes"
               endif
               x = x + 1
          endwhile
          pairsToCompare = pairsToCompare - 1
     endwhile
return

switchValues()
     temp = score[x+1]
     score[x+1] = score[x]
     score[x] = temp
return



// This is the work of the sortScores() module.
pairsToCompare = numberOfEls -1; // Number of items to compare.
switchOccurred = true;  // Set flag to true.
// Outer loop controls number of passes over data.
while(switchOccurred == true) // Test flag.
{
     x = 0;
     switchOccurred = false;
     // Inner loop controls number of items to compare.
     while(x < pairsToCompare)
     {
          if(score[x] > score[x+1]) // Swap?
          {
               // This is the work done in the switchValues() module.
               temp = score[x+1];
               score[x+1] = score[x];
               score[x] = temp;
               switchOccurred = true;
          }
          x++;   // Get ready for next pair.
     }
     pairsToCompare--;  // Reduce number of items to compare.
}
```

Within the inner loop you compare adjacent items in the array using the subscript variable **x** and **x+1** to see if you should swap them. If the values should be swapped, you use the technique discussed earlier to rearrange the two values in the array. The last thing you do in the inner loop is add one to the value of the subscript variable x. You do this because you want to compare the next two adjacent items in the array the next time the inner loop executes. You continue to compare two adjacent items and possibly swap them as long as the value of x is less than the value of `pairsToCompare`. Notice that the comparison made as part of the inner loop, `x<pairsToCompare`, uses the less than operator, <, not the <= operator that is used in the pseudocode. You must do this because you would compare too many items using <= because Java subscripts begin with 0, not 1.

THE FINISHUP() MODULE

In the `finishUp()` module, you output the sorted array, close the input file, and exit the program. Figure 7-4 includes the pseudocode and the Java code that implements the work done in the `finishUp()` module.

FIGURE 7-4: WORK DONE IN `finishUp()` MODULE

```
finishUp()
     x = 1
     while x <= numberOfEls
           print score[x]
           x = x + 1
     endwhile
     close files
return


// This is the work of the finishUp() module.
x = 0;  // Reset array subscript.
// Print items in array that are now sorted.
while(x < numberOfEls)
{
     System.out.println(score[x]);
     x++;
}

br.close(); // Close input file.
// Exit the program.
System.exit(0);
```

As you can see in Figure 7-4, you must first assign a new value to the subscript variable, x. In the pseudocode, you assign the value 1 to x, but in the Java code, you assign the value 0. Again, this is because you want to assign the first subscript value to x. You then use a loop to print all of the values in the array named `score` by incrementing the value of the subscript variable, x, each time the loop body executes. Finally, you close the input file and exit the program.

EXERCISE 7-2: USING A BUBBLE SORT

In this exercise, you use what you have learned about sorting data using a bubble sort. Study the following Java code, and then answer the subsequent questions.

```
int numbers[] = {3, 22, -1, 44, 121, 200, 15, 55};
int numItems = 8;
```

```
int j, k, temp;
int numPasses = 0, numCompares = 0, numSwaps = 0;
for(j = 0; j < numItems - 1; j++)
{
    numPasses++;
    for(k = 0; k < numItems - 1; k++)
    {
        numCompares++;
        if(numbers[k] > numbers[k+1])
        {
            numSwaps++;
            temp = numbers[k+1];
            numbers[k+1] = numbers[k];
            numbers[k] = temp;
        }
    }
}
```

1. Does this code perform an ascending sort or a descending sort? How do you know?

   _____

2. How many passes are made over the data in the array? Specify a number, such as 3.

   _____

3. How many comparisons are made? Specify a number, such as 35.

   _____

4. Do the variables named **numPasses**, **numCompares**, and **numSwaps** accurately keep track of the number of passes, compares, and swaps made in this bubble sort? Explain your answer.

   _____

LAB 7-2: USING A BUBBLE SORT

In this lab, you complete a partially prewritten Java program that uses an array to store data for the Hinner College Foundation. The program is described in Chapter 9, Exercise 2 in *Programming Logic and Design*. The program should output the highest five donations. Read the problem description carefully and look over the input file, **donations.dat**, before you begin. Variables have been declared and values have been read from the input file and stored in parallel arrays.

In this lab, you sort the donation amounts in descending order using a bubble sort. Also, when you swap a donation amount, remember to swap the donor name as well. Finally, you should print the five highest donation amounts. Note that there are comments in the code that tell you where to write your statements.

1. Open the source code file named **Donations.java** using Notepad or the text editor of your choice.

2. Write the bubble sort.

3. Output the five highest donation amounts along with the donor names.

4. Save this source code file in a directory of your choice, and then make that directory your working directory.

5. Compile the source code file, `Donations.java`.

6. Execute the program and record the output.

MULTIDIMENSIONAL ARRAYS

A **multidimensional array** stores data items that require multiple subscripts to access them. In Chapter 9 of *Programming Logic and Design*, you learned that if you want to represent values in a table or a grid that contains rows and columns, you might want to use a **two-dimensional array**. Each element in a two-dimensional array requires two subscripts to reference it. One subscript is used to reference the row, and the second subscript is used to reference the column.

The rent-determining program described in Chapter 9 in *Programming Logic and Design* uses a two-dimensional array to represent the rent charged for apartments in an apartment building. The floor on which the apartment is located and the number of bedrooms in the apartment are both necessary to determine the rent. The Java code that follows declares a two-dimensional array of data type `double` to store the rent amounts:

```
double rent[][] = new double[5][3];
```

You begin by specifying the data type (`double`), the name of the array (`rent`), and then use two pairs of square brackets to tell the compiler that this array has two dimensions. On the right side of the assignment operator, you use the `new` operator to instruct the compiler to allocate memory for an array of data type `double` that has 5 rows and 3 columns.

TIP □ □ □ □ | The number of rows is specified first, then the number of columns.

The preceding two-dimensional array is shown in Figure 7-5.

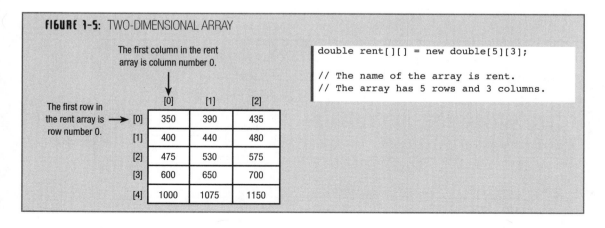

FIGURE 7-5: TWO-DIMENSIONAL ARRAY

The first column in the rent array is column number 0.

The first row in the rent array is row number 0.

```
double rent[][] = new double[5][3];

// The name of the array is rent.
// The array has 5 rows and 3 columns.
```

	[0]	[1]	[2]
[0]	350	390	435
[1]	400	440	480
[2]	475	530	575
[3]	600	650	700
[4]	1000	1075	1150

As you know, you must use two subscript values to access a single item in the array named `rent`. For example, `rent[0][1]` accesses the value 390, which is stored in the first row and the second column of the array.

The Java code that follows illustrates how you can use nested `for` loops to access all of the elements of the two-dimensional array named `rent`:

```
int numRows = 5, numColumns = 3;
double rent[][] = new double[numRows][numColumns];
int floor, numberOfBedrooms;
for(floor = 0; floor < numRows; floor++)
    for(numberOfBedrooms = 0; numberOfBedrooms < numColumns;
                                    numberOfBedrooms++)
        System.out.println("Rent: " +
                    rent[floor][numberOfBedrooms]);
```

In the preceding Java code you declare two `int` variables named `numRows` and `numColumns`. These variables are initialized to the number of rows in the array (5) and the number of columns in the array (3). You use these variables when you declare the array and to control the loops. You also declare two `int` variables, `floor` and `numberOfBedrooms`. The outer loop uses the subscript variable named `floor` to control access to the rows in the array. The inner loop uses the subscript variable named `numberOfBedrooms` to access the columns in the array. You use both subscripts to access a data item in the array in the `System.out.println()` statement.

Note that a complete Java program using the `rent` array is written and stored in the file named `Rent.java`. You can compile and execute this program to see how the program behaves.

EXERCISE 7-3: USING MULTIDIMENSIONAL ARRAYS

In this exercise, you use what you have learned about multidimensional arrays to answer the questions that follow. You have been asked to write a program for the Build-Rite Manufacturing Company that calculates shipping charges for orders. All orders are charged a basic shipping rate of $20, plus an additional charge based on the quantity of items shipped and the destination. The shipping rates are shown in Table 7-1.

TABLE 7-1: SHIPPING RATES

Quantity	Region 1	Region 2	Region 3	Region 4	Region 5
1	1.00	2.00	3.00	4.00	5.00
2	2.00	4.00	6.00	8.00	10.00
3	2.50	4.50	6.50	8.50	10.50
4	3.00	5.00	7.00	9.00	11.00
5	3.25	5.25	7.25	9.25	11.25
More than 5	3.50	5.50	7.50	9.50	11.50

1. Declare a two-dimensional array named `rates` to store the shipping rates.

   _____

2. How much will a customer pay to ship 3 items to Region 3?

   _____

3. You want to change the shipping rate for 4 items shipped to Region 2 from 5.00 to 5.25. Write the Java statement that accomplishes this task.

   _____

4. Write the Java code that prints all the rates stored in the two-dimensional array.

   _____

   _____

   _____

LAB 7-3: USING MULTIDIMENSIONAL ARRAYS

In this lab, you use what you have learned about multidimensional arrays to complete a partially prewritten Java program written for the Family Fun Golf Park. The program is described in Chapter 9, Exercise 9 in *Programming Logic and Design*. The program should output the name of a golfer, his or her score on each of the nine holes, and one of the following phrases: "Over par", "Par", or "Under par".

Read the problem description carefully before you begin. Variables have been declared, but you must write the assignment statements to populate the 2D array of pars for each age group. Input statements that ask the user to input a golfer's name, age, and scores for each of nine holes have also been done for you. You must print the golfer's name and age, print each of the nine scores for that golfer, and then determine which phrase, "Over par", "Par", or "Under par", should be printed, given the golfer's age and score. There are comments in the code that tell you where to write your statements. You can use the Rent program in this chapter as a guide.

1. Open the source code file named `Golf.java` using Notepad or the text editor of your choice.
2. Study the prewritten code to understand what has already been done.
3. Use assignment statements to populate the two-dimensional array.
4. Print the golfer's name and age.
5. Write a loop statement that allows you to compare each of the golfer's scores with the par values stored in the two-dimensional array to see if the score is "Under par", "Par", or "Over par". Use the golfer's age and the hole number to access the two-dimensional array.
6. Save this source code file in a directory of your choice, and then make that directory your working directory.
7. Compile the source code file, `Golf.java`.

8. Execute the program using the following as input:

   Golfer Name: `Freda Kozinski`

   Age: `13`

   Scores: `6    3    6    4    5    3    5    5    4`

9. Confirm that your output matches the following:

   Name: Freda Kozinski

   Age: 13

   Hole 1 Score 6 Over par

   Hole 2 Score 3 Under par

   Hole 3 Score 6 Over par

   Hole 4 Score 4 Par

   Hole 5 Score 5 Over par

   Hole 6 Score 3 Under par

   Hole 7 Score 5 Over par

   Hole 8 Score 5 Over par

   Hole 9 Score 4 Par

8

USING MENUS AND PERFORMING DATA VALIDATION

After studying Chapter 8, you will be able to:

- ☐ Use Java's `switch` statement
- ☐ Write menu-driven programs in Java
- ☐ Validate user input in interactive programs

In Chapter 10, you learned that **interactive** programs depend on getting input from a user while the program is running. You also learned that a **menu program** is one in which the user is presented with options and is expected to choose from those options in real time. **Real time** means as the program is running. In addition, you found out that menu programs rely on a user to enter data, and because you cannot be sure that users enter valid data, you must validate the user's input. **Validating input** means to check the input to be sure your program can use it. It is recommended that you do the exercises and labs in this chapter only after you have finished Chapter 10 of *Programming Logic and Design*.

In this chapter, you learn how to write interactive, menu-driven programs that use a `switch` statement. Using the `switch` statement allows you to write programs that are easier to read and maintain. Because your programs now rely on users to enter input, you also see how to validate their input in your programs by using a variety of methods.

Let's begin by looking at the `switch` statement.

 | Chapter 8 of this text corresponds to Chapter 10 in *Programming Logic and Design, Third Edition, Comprehensive*. If you are using *Programming Logic and Design, Third Edition, Introductory*, you have only Chapters 1–8. Nonetheless, the chapter you are about to read has been provided to you as a bridge to further study. If necessary, your instructor can provide you with the corresponding chapter from the Logic Comprehensive text.

THE SWITCH STATEMENT

The `switch` statement is similar to a nested `if` statement because it is also a multipath decision statement. A `switch` statement offers the advantage of being more readable than nested `if` statements, and a `switch` statement is also easier for a programmer to maintain. You use the `switch` statement in situations when you want to compare an expression with several integer constants.

The syntax (or rules) for writing a `switch` statement in Java is as follows:

```
switch(expression)
{
   case constant: statement(s);
   case constant: statement(s);
   case constant: statement(s);
   default:       statement(s);
}
```

You begin writing a `switch` statement with the keyword `switch`. Then, within parentheses, you include an expression that evaluates to an integer constant. Cases are then defined within the `switch` statement by using the keyword `case` as a label, and including an integer constant after this label. For example, you could include an integer constant such as 10 or an arithmetic expression that evaluates to an integer such as 10/2. The computer evaluates the expression in the `switch` statement and then compares it to the integer constants following the `case` labels. If the expression and the integer value match, then the computer executes the statement(s) that follow until it encounters a `break` statement or a closing curly brace. The `break` statement causes an exit from the `switch` statement. You can use the keyword `default` to establish a case for values that do not match any of the integer values following the `case` labels. Note also that all of the cases, including the default case, are enclosed within curly braces.

TIP ▫ ▫ ▫ ▫ | If you omit a **break** statement in a **case**, all the code up to the next **break** statement or a closing curly brace is executed. This is probably not what you intend.

The following code sample illustrates the use of the **switch** statement in Java:

```java
int deptNum;
String deptName;
deptNum = 2;
switch(deptNum)
{
     case 1:     deptName = "Marketing";
                 break;
     case 2:     deptName = "Development";
                 break;
     case 3:     deptName = "Sales";
                 break;
     default:    deptName = "Unknown";
                 break;
}
System.out.println("Department: " + deptName);
```

When the **switch** statement is encountered in the preceding Java code, the value of the variable named **deptNum** is 2. The value 2 matches the integer constant 2 in the second case of the **switch** statement. Therefore, the String constant "Development" is assigned to the **String** variable named **deptName**. A **break** statement is encountered next, and causes an exit from the **switch** statement. The statement following the **switch** statement **System.out.println("Department: " + deptName);** executes next.

EXERCISE 8-1: USING A SWITCH STATEMENT

In this exercise, you use what you have learned about the switch statement to study some Java code, and then you answer the questions that follow.

First, examine the following code:

```java
int number;
int result = 0;
switch(number)
{
   case 1:  result += 1;
   case 2:  result += 2;
   case 3:  result += 3;
            break;
   case 4:  result += 4;
   case 5:  result += 5;
```

```
        default: result = 0;
                break;
    }
    System.out.println("Result: " + result);
```

1. What is the value of `result` if the value of `number` is 2?

_____

2. What is the value of `result` if the value of `number` is 1?

_____

3. What is the value of `result` if the value of `number` is 4?

_____

4. What is the value of `result` if the value of `number` is 12?

_____

5. Is the `break` statement in the `default` case needed? Explain.

_____

LAB 8-1: USING A SWITCH STATEMENT

In this lab, you complete a prewritten Java program that calculates an employee's end-of-year bonus and prints the employee's name, yearly salary, performance rating, and bonus. This is the same program you wrote in Lab 3-3 when you used nested `if` statements to write the program. This time you use a `switch` statement instead of nested `if` statements.

In this program, bonuses are calculated based on employees' annual salary and their performance rating. The rating system is contained in Table 8-1:

TABLE 8-1: EMPLOYEE RATINGS AND BONUSES

Rating	Bonus
1	6 percent of annual salary
2	4 percent of annual salary
3	2 percent of annual salary
4	None

1. Open the file named `Lab8_1.java` using Notepad or the text editor of your choice.
2. Variables have been declared for you and the input statements and output statements have been written. Read them over carefully before you proceed to the next step.
3. Design the logic and write the rest of the program using a `switch` statement.
4. Compile the program.

5. Execute the program entering the following as input:

Employee's name: **Frances Williams**

Employee's salary: **45000.00**

Employee's performance rating: **2**

6. Confirm that your output matches the following:

Employee Name Frances Williams

Employee Salary $45000.0

Employee Rating 2

Employee Bonus $1800.0

TIP □ □ □ □ | You cannot control the number of places that appear after the decimal point until you learn more about Java.

WRITING MENU-DRIVEN PROGRAMS IN JAVA

In Chapter 10 of *Programming Logic and Design*, you studied the logic for an educational program that drills a user on elementary arithmetic skills. You also learned that you can write a menu-driven program as a **console application**, requiring the user to enter choices using the keyboard, or as a **graphical user interface** application, allowing the user to use a mouse or pointing device to make choices.

Using Java, you can write either of these types of menu-driven programs. However, in this chapter, you write console applications that use dialog boxes rather than full-blown graphical user interfaces. You do not know enough about Java (yet) to write a graphical user interface program.

The mainline logic for the arithmetic drill menu program includes performing the `startUp()` module, followed by a `while` loop that continues as long as the user does not want to quit the program. Within the `while` loop, the `looping()` module is performed. After the loop, the `cleanUp()` module is performed. This is shown in Figure 8-1. Note that the complete arithmetic drill menu program written in Java is stored in the file named `Arithmetic.java`.

FIGURE 8-1: MAINLINE LOGIC FOR ARITHMETIC DRILL MENU PROGRAM

```
start
     perform startUp()
     while response not = 3
          perform looping()
     endwhile
     perform cleanUp()
stop
```

Next, you look at the logic for each of the modules separately. Note, however, that all of the code for the work done in these modules is written in the `main()` method in our Java programs.

THE STARTUP( ) MODULE

The work done in the `startUp( )` module includes declaring variables, opening files, and performing the `displayMenu( )` module. Figure 8-2 includes the pseudocode and the Java code that implements the work done in the `startUp( )` module and the `displayMenu( )` module.

FIGURE 8-2: WORK DONE IN `startUp( )` AND `displayMenu( )` MODULES

```
startUp()
     declare variables
     open files
     perform displayMenu()
return

displayMenu()
     print "(1) Addition Problems"
     print "(2) Subtraction Problems"
     print "(3) Quit the Program"
     print "Please press a number to make your selection"
     read response
return



// This is the work done in startUp().
// Declare variables.
String responseString;   // String version of user's menu response.
int response = 3;        // User's response initialized to 3 (quit).
int errorCount = 0;      // Keep track of incorrect user responses.
int count;               // Keep track of number of problems.
int first;               // First number between 1 and 10.
int second;              // Second number between 1 and 10.
int answer;              // User's answer to arithmetic problem.
String answerString;     // String version of user's answer.

// Display menu and get user input.
responseString = JOptionPane.showInputDialog("(1) Addition Problems" +
     "\n(2) Subtraction Problems" + "\n(3) Quit the Program" +
     "\n\nPlease press a number to make your selection.");
// Convert from String to int.
response = Integer.parseInt(responseString);
```

As you can see in Figure 8-2, variables are declared first. The second step is to open input files. You do not need to implement this step because this program does not require input files. Next, you perform the `displayMenu( )` module.

By now, you should be familiar with the `showInputDialog( )` method. In this program, you use the `showInputDialog( )` method to display the menu. Notice that the newline character, `\n`, is embedded in the string constants you use in the `showInputDialog( )` method. You do this to force the three options in your menu to appear on separate lines. Also notice that you use two newline characters to separate the menu options from your directions to the user. As you have learned, the `showInputDialog( )` method returns a `String` that contains your user's choice from the menu. You assign your user's choice to the `String` variable named responseString. Next, you use the `parseInt()` method to convert the `String` to an `int` and assign the `int` to the variable named `response`.

Now that you have your user's first choice from the menu, you are ready to write the `looping()` module.

THE LOOPING( ) MODULE

As long as your user does not choose to quit the program (choice number 3 on your menu), the `looping()` module executes. Figure 8-3 includes the pseudocode for the work done in the `looping()` module as well as the `addition()` and `subtraction()` modules. Figure 8-4 includes the Java code that implements the `looping()`, `addition()`, and `subtraction()` modules.

FIGURE 8-3: PSEUDOCODE FOR `looping()`, `addition()`, AND `subtraction()` MODULES

```
looping()
   if response = 1 then
      perform addition()
      errorCount = 0
   else
      if response = 2 then
         perform subtraction()
         errorCount = 0
      else
         errorCount = errorCount + 1
         if errorCount > 2 then
            print "Please see the system administrator for help"
         else
            print "You must select 1, 2, or 3"
         endif
      endif
   endif
   perform displayMenu()
return

addition()
   count = 1
   while count < 5
      first = random(10)
      second = random(10)
      print first, "+", second, " ?"
      read response
      if response = first + second then
         print "Right"
      else
         print "Wrong"
      endif
      count = count + 1
   endwhile
return
```

FIGURE 8-3: PSEUDOCODE FOR `looping()`, `addition()`, AND `subtraction()` MODULES (CONTINUED)

```
subtraction()
   count = 1
   while count < 5
      first = random(10)
      second = random(10)
      print first, "-", second, " ?"
      read response
      if response = first - second then
         print "Right"
      else
         print "Wrong"
      endif
      count = count + 1
   endwhile
return
```

FIGURE 8-4: JAVA CODE FOR `looping()`, `addition()`, AND `subtraction()` MODULES

```
// This is the work done in looping(), addition() and subtraction().
// As long as the user does not want to quit (3).
while(response != 3)
{
   switch(response)
   {
      case 1:    // This is the work done in addition().
                 count = 1;
                 while(count < 5) // Generate 4 problems.
                 {
                    // Get random numbers between 1 and 10.
                    first = 1 + (int) (Math.random() * 10 );
                    second = 1 + (int) (Math.random() * 10 );
                    // Display problem and get user's answer.
                    answerString = JOptionPane.showInputDialog(first +
                             " + " + second + "= ?");
                    // Convert  answer to int.
                    answer = Integer.parseInt(answerString);
                    // Test to see if answer is correct.
                    if(answer == (first + second))
                       JOptionPane.showMessageDialog(null, "Right");
                    else
                       JOptionPane.showMessageDialog(null, "Wrong");
                    // Next problem.
                    count++;
                 }
                 // User did not make incorrect choice from menu.
                 errorCount = 0;
                 break;
```

FIGURE 8-4: JAVA CODE FOR `looping()`, `addition()`, AND `subtraction()` MODULES (CONTINUED)

```java
      case 2:    // This is the work done in subtraction().
                 count = 1;
                 while(count < 5) // Generate 4 problems.
                 {
                     // Get random numbers between 1 and 10.
                     first = 1 + (int) (Math.random() * 10 );
                     second = 1 + (int) (Math.random() * 10 );
                     // Display problem and get user's answer.
                     answerString = JOptionPane.showInputDialog(first +
                                 " - " + second + "= ?");
                     // Convert answer to int.
                     answer = Integer.parseInt(answerString);
                     // Test to see if answer is correct.
                     if(answer == (first - second))
                         JOptionPane.showMessageDialog(null, "Right");
                     else
                         JOptionPane.showMessageDialog(null, "Wrong");
                     // Next problem.
                     count++;
                 }
                 // User did not make incorrect choice from menu.
                 errorCount = 0;
                 break;
      default:   // Add one to number of user errors.
                 errorCount++;
                 // Allow 3 incorrect choices, then stronger message.
                 if(errorCount > 2)
                     JOptionPane.showMessageDialog(null,
                         "Please see the system administrator for help.");
                 else
                     JOptionPane.showMessageDialog(null,
                         "You must select 1, 2, or 3.");
      } // End of switch.
      // Display menu again and get user input.
      responseString = JOptionPane.showInputDialog("(1)Addition Problems"
              + "\n(2)Subtraction Problems" + "\n(3)Quit the Program" +
              "\n\nPlease press a number to make your selection.");
      response = Integer.parseInt(responseString);
}
```

As shown in Figure 8-4, you use a `switch` statement to determine whether your user wants to practice addition or subtraction or has entered an incorrect choice from the menu. In the `switch` statement, the value of the `int` variable named `response` is compared to the integer constants 1 and 2. If the value of `response` is 1, the code following `case 1:` executes. If the value of `response` is 2, the code following `case 2:` executes. And if the value of `response` is neither 1 nor 2, the code written for the `default` case is executed.

The code written for `case 1:` is actually the work done in the `addition()` module. This includes generating four addition problems for your user to answer. You use the variable `count` to keep track of how many addition problems to generate and begin by assigning the value 1 to `count`. You then use a `while` loop that includes the expression `count < 5`. This loop will execute 4 times, once for each addition problem.

To determine the numbers to include in the addition problem, you use Java's `random()` method. The `random()` method belongs to the `Math` class. When you want to use it, you write the name the class followed by a dot (`.`) and then the name of the method. This is shown in the code that follows:

```
first = 1 + (int)(Math.random() * 10);
second = 1 + (int)(Math.random() * 10);
```

The `random()` method generates a floating point number (data type `double`) from 0.0 up to, but not including 1.0. Because you want to generate numbers between 1 and 10, you multiply the value generated by `random()` by the number `10`. The result of the multiplication is a value that has data type `double`. To change this `double` to an `int` and **truncate**, or get rid of, the part after the decimal point, you use a type cast. A **type cast** is used to transform any data type into another data type. The `(int)` that precedes `(Math.random() * 10)` causes the `double` returned by the `random()` method and multiplied by `10` to be transformed into an `int`. Finally, you add one to the `int`, because you want numbers between 1 and 10, not numbers between 0 and 9.

You then use the `showInputDialog()` method to show the user the problem in a dialog box. Your user provides an answer in the text area of the dialog box, and then this value is assigned to the `String` variable `answerString`. You use the `parseInt()` method to convert `answerString` to an `int`, and then assign the `int` to the variable named `answer`.

You use the statement `if(answer == first + second)` to test whether your user provided the correct answer. If the answer is correct, you use the `showMessageDialog()` method to display "`Right`" in a message dialog box. If the answer is not correct, you display "`Wrong`" in a message dialog box.

The `showMessageDialog()` method is new to you, but it is similar to the `showInputDialog()` method you already know. Both methods belong to the `JOptionPane` class and are invoked by naming the `JOptionPane` class followed by a `.` (dot), followed by the name of the method. Instead of always displaying output in the DOS window on your user's screen, you can use the `showMessageDialog()` method to display output to the user in a dialog box. You must include two pieces of information, called **arguments**, separated by a comma when you use this method. The first argument is the keyword `null`. This tells Java to display the dialog box in the middle of the screen. The second argument is the string you want shown in the dialog box. This can be a `String` object or a string constant.

After you display the message dialog box, you increment the variable named `count` and then repeat the loop that displays three more addition problems. Once you have displayed all four addition problems, you exit the loop and set `errorCount` to 0. You do this to indicate that the user did not make an incorrect choice from the menu. You include the `break` statement as the last statement in the code for `case 1:` in order to break out of the `switch` statement.

The code written for `case 2:` is the work done in the `subtraction()` module. It is identical to the code for `case 1:`, except that you use the subtraction operator in the statement `if(answer == (first - second))`, and you use the – character in the string argument to the `showInputDialog()` method `answerString = JOptionPane.showInputDialog(first + " - " + second + "= ?");`.

In the default case, you add one to `errorCount` to keep track of the number of incorrect choices your user makes when selecting an option from the menu. If the value of `errorCount` is greater than 2, you use the `showMessageDialog()` method again, this time to display the stronger message `"Please see the system administrator for help."`. If the value of `errorCount` is 2 or less, you use the `showMessageDialog()` method to display the regular message `"You must select 1, 2 or 3."`.

After the `switch` statement, you display the menu again, get your user's choice using the `showInputDialog()` method, convert your user's answer to an `int`, and then repeat the outer loop until your user chooses 3 from the menu. Choosing 3 means your user wants to quit the arithmetic drill program.

THE CLEANUP( ) MODULE

In the `cleanUp()` module, you use the `showMessageDialog()` method again, this time to show your user a goodbye message and then exit the program.

EXERCISE 8-2: USING MENU-DRIVEN PROGRAMS

In this exercise, you use what you have learned about menu-driven programs to answer the questions that follow.

1. How many options should you provide on a menu for a program that allows a user to take a trivia quiz? When taking the quiz, the user may choose trivia questions about movies, television, or sports. Explain why you need each option.

   _____

2. You are developing a program that allows a user to enter up to 50 integer values. After the integer values are entered, the user may then ask for the minimum value in the list of integers, the maximum value, the mean value, or the median value. You want to use a menu in this program. How many options will you provide on the menu? Explain why you need each option.

   _____

3. Do you consider well-designed, menu-driven programs to be more user-friendly than programs that do not include a menu? Explain your answer.

   _____

   _____

4. When you write menu-driven programs, the `switch` statement provides you a more convenient way to test a series of values.

    a. Do you agree that using a `switch` statement is more convenient? Explain.

    _____

    b. What is another statement you can use to test a series of values?

    _____

5. Describe a situation in which you would not be able to use a `switch` statement even though you have a series of values to test.

    _____

LAB 8-2: MENU-DRIVEN PROGRAMS

In this lab, you complete a partially prewritten, menu-driven Java program for a fast-food restaurant. The program is described in Chapter 10, Exercise 4, in *Programming Logic and Design*. The program should allow a customer to keep ordering from the menu described until they press 4 for End Order, at which point you should display the total amount of the order. Read the problem description before you begin. Variables have been declared for you. There are comments in the code that tell you where to write your statements.

Open the source code file named `Menu.java` using Notepad or the text editor of your choice.

1. Write the code that displays a menu and allows your user to choose an option from the menu until he or she wants to end the order.
2. Calculate the amount of the bill and display it in a message dialog box.
3. Save this source code file in a directory of your choice, and then make that directory your working directory.
4. Compile the source code file, `Menu.java`.
5. Execute the program with the following input:
    a. 2 Hot Dogs, 1 Fries, 1 Lemonade
    b. 1 Hot Dog, 2 Fries
    c. Nothing, Choose 4 (End Order) from the menu
    d. 1 Hot Dog, 2 Lemonade
    e. 2 Fries, 1 Hot Dog, 2 Lemonade

VALIDATING INPUT

In Chapter 10 of *Programming Logic and Design*, you learned that you cannot count on users to enter valid data in menu-driven programs and in programs that ask the user to enter data. You also learned that you should validate input from your user so you can avoid problems caused by invalid input. Validating input can include testing for an exact match, testing for a particular data type, testing to see if input values fall within a range of values, testing to see if input values are reasonable, and testing to see if input values are present. The following sections discuss each test.

TESTING FOR AN EXACT MATCH

If your program requires a user to enter a specific value, such as a "Y" or an "N" in response to a question, then your program should validate that your user entered an exact match to either "Y" or "N". If not, you must decide what action to take in your program. As an example of testing for an exact match, consider the following code:

```
String answer;
answer =
  JOptionPane.showInputDialog("Do you want to continue?"
     + " Enter Y or N.");
while((answer.compareTo("Y") != 0) &&
      (answer.compareTo("N") != 0))
{
   answer =
     JOptionPane.showInputDialog("Invalid Response." +
       " Please type Y or N.");
}
```

In the example, the variable named `answer` contains your user's answer to the question `"Do you want to continue? Enter Y or N."`. In the expression that is part of the `while` loop, you use the `compareTo()` method test to see if your user entered a `"Y"` or an `"N"`. If not, you enter the loop, tell the user he or she entered invalid input, and then request that he or she type a `"Y"` or an "N". The expression in the `while` loop is tested again to see if your user entered valid data this time. If not, the loop body executes again and continues to execute until the user enters valid input.

TIP □ □ □ □ | Remember that you use the `compareTo()` method to compare `Strings`.

Now, let's see how to validate a data type.

VALIDATING A DATA TYPE

In Java, you can check data items entered by a user to make sure they are the correct data type. For example, if you asked your user to enter a salary, you should make sure the data value entered is numeric before you use the `parseDouble()` method to convert a `String` to a `double`. If you try to convert a `String` to a `double` and the `String` does not contain numeric characters or a single decimal point, an exception occurs in your program, and your program stops executing. The following code sample illustrates a technique you can use to determine if characters in a `String` object are numeric:

```
String salString;
double salary;
```

```
int i;
int count = 0;
salString =
      JOptionPane.showInputDialog("Enter a salary.");
i = 0;
while(i < salString.length())
{
   if(Character.isDigit(salString.charAt(i)))
      i++;
   else if(salString.charAt(i) == '.' && count == 0)
   {
       count++;
       i++;
   }
   else
   {
      JOptionPane.showMessageDialog(null,
                            "Invalid input.");
      salString =
        JOptionPane.showInputDialog("Enter a salary.");
       i = 0;
       count = 0;
   }
}
salary = Double.parseDouble(salString);
JOptionPane.showMessageDialog(null, "Salary: " +
      salary);
```

In the example, the `String` variable `salString` contains your user's input. You need to test each character in the `String` to see if it is a number or a decimal point and to make sure that there is only one decimal point in the `String`. You can use a method named `isDigit()` that belongs to the `Character` class to test whether a single character is a digit. The digit characters are 0, 1, 2, 3, 4, 5, 6, 7, 8, or 9. You can test for the decimal point (period) simply by using the equality operator `(==)`, but you will also have to use a counter variable to be sure there is just one decimal point in your user's input. You must use a loop to be able to check each character. You do this using a technique similar to how you loop through an array. It is similar because the first position in a `String` is position 0, as it is in an array, but you access individual elements using the `String` method `charAt()`. When you use the `charAt()` method, you include the position number in the `String` within parentheses rather than using a subscript.

A problem you sometimes face is that you don't know how many characters there are in the `String` object. Therefore, you don't know how to set up the loop. Fortunately, you can use a method that belongs to the `String` class called `length()` to find out how many characters are in a `String` object. If you set up the loop as shown in `while(i < salString.length())`, you can access the `String` at position 0 by using `charAt(i)` and continue to access each element of the `String` as long as i is less than the length of the `String`.

In the body of the `while` loop, you use the `isDigit()` method to test if the character in the `String` at the position represented by the value of `i` is a digit. The `isDigit()` method returns the value `true` if the character is a digit, and `false` if it isn't, so it is natural to use this method in an `if` statement. If the character is a digit, you increment `i` to get ready to test the next character in the `String`.

If the character is not a digit, you then test to see if the character at position `i` is a decimal point (`.`) and if this is the first decimal point in the user's input. You use an else if statement along with AND logic for this test because both conditions must be true for the input to be valid. The first test in the else if statement is carried out by using the equality operator (`==`) and enclosing the period (`.`) in single quotation marks. In Java, single quotation marks are used for a constant made of a single character. The second test is carried out by using the equality operator (`==`) to see if the value of the variable named `count` is equal to `0`. The variable named count is initialized to contain the value `0` and if its value is still `0` when the else if statement executes, you know that this is the first decimal point you have encountered in your user's input. If both of these tests result in a true value, you increment your counter variable, `count`, because now you have encountered a decimal point and you also increment `i` to get ready to test the next character in the `String`.

If the character is not a digit or a decimal point or if the character is not the first decimal point, then it is an invalid character. You use the `showMessageDialog()` method to tell your user that he or she entered invalid data. You then use the `showInputDialog()` method to ask the user to enter a salary again. You also set the loop control variable, `i`, and the counter variable, `count`, back to `0`. This allows you to begin testing the new input entered by the user.

Once you are sure your user has entered valid data, you use the `parseDouble()` method to convert `salString` to a `double` and assign it to the variable named `salary`. Lastly, you display the value of `salary` in a message dialog box.

The complete program is in the file named `ValidateDataType.java`. You may want to compile and run the program to observe its behavior.

Next, we look at validating a data range.

VALIDATING A DATA RANGE

If you ask your user to enter a numeric value to represent a month, then you should validate that the user's response falls within the range of values 1 to 12. A correct response from your user can be any number within that range. The following code sample illustrates how you do this in Java:

```java
String monthString;
int month;
int i;
monthString =
    JOptionPane.showInputDialog("Enter month.");
i = 0;
while(i < monthString.length())
{
    if(Character.isDigit(monthString.charAt(i)))
        i++;
```

```java
        else
        {
            JOptionPane.showMessageDialog(null,
                    "Invalid Input.");
            monthString =
                    JOptionPane.showInputDialog("Enter month.");
            i = 0;
        }
    }
    month = Integer.parseInt(monthString);
    while(month < 1 || month > 12)
    {
        monthString =
         JOptionPane.showInputDialog("Invalid response."+
            " Please enter month 1 through 12.");
        i = 0;
        while(i < monthString.length())
        {
            if(Character.isDigit(monthString.charAt(i)))
                i++;
            else
            {
                JOptionPane.showMessageDialog(null,
                    "Invalid Input.");
                monthString = JOptionPane.showInputDialog(
                    "Enter month.");
                i = 0;
            }
        }
        month = Integer.parseInt(monthString);
    }
    JOptionPane.showMessageDialog(null, "Month: "
            + month);
```

In the example, the `String` variable named `monthString` contains your user's input. Before you convert this `String` to an `int`, you validate the data type of the input, as you learned in the previous section. If the input is made up of digit characters, you convert it to an `int` and assign it to the variable named `month`. You then use an OR expression and the OR operator (`||`) in a `while` loop to test if the `int` variable `month` is less than 1 or greater than 12. If it is, you tell your user to try again, after having entered invalid input.

The complete program is in the file named `ValidateRange.java`. You may want to compile and run the program to observe its behavior.

Next, you see how to test for reasonableness and consistency in data entered by your user.

VALIDATING REASONABLENESS AND CONSISTENCY OF DATA

Sometimes when you write a program, you need to do more than test to see if user input is the correct data type or falls within a range of values. For example, the business rules for a pharmaceutical company state that a product in Category A can never cost less than $5.00 or more than $10.00. If you write a program for this company that allows clerical personnel to enter new products and prices into their database, you would have to validate that if the product category is A, then the cost entered cannot be less than $5.00 or more than $10.00. If this were allowed, the company's data would be inconsistent with their business rules. To write this program, you need knowledge of how Java can be used to interact with a database, which is beyond the scope of this book.

VALIDATING THE PRESENCE OF DATA

In a previous example, you looked at some Java code that used the `showInputDialog()` method to ask a user to enter a salary. In Java, when an input dialog box appears, it is possible that your user will not enter anything at all. Instead, he or she might press Enter or click OK. Because of this possibility, you should test for the presence of data before you continue with your program. The following code sample illustrates how you do this in Java:

```
salString =
        JOptionPane.showInputDialog("Enter a salary.");
while(salString.compareTo("") == 0)
{
    salString =
            JOptionPane.showInputDialog("Enter a salary.");
}
```

In the example, the `String` variable named `salString` contains your user's input. The expression in the `while` loop compares the value of `salString` with the string constant " ". In Java, the string constant " " is called the **null string**. This is a string that contains no characters. The value of `salString` would be null if the user pressed Enter or clicked OK instead of entering data in the input dialog box. If your user does not enter data in the input dialog box, the loop body continues to execute, asking the user to enter a salary. Of course, once the user enters some data, it may have to be validated using the methods discussed previously.

EXERCISE 8-3: VALIDATING USER INPUT

In this exercise, you use what you learned about validating user input to answer the following questions:

1. You plan to use the following statement in a Java program to validate user input:

   ```
   while(userInput.compareTo("") == 0)
   ```

   What would your user enter to cause this test to be `true`?

   _____

2. You plan to use the following statement in a Java program to validate user input:

   ```
   while((userAnswer.compareTo("N") == 0) &&
   (userAnswer.compareTo("Y") == 0))
   ```

What would a user enter to cause this test to be `true`?

_____

3. You plan to use the following statement in a Java program to validate user input:

```
while(userAnswer < 5 || userAnswer > 10)
```

What would a user enter to cause this test to be `true`?

_____

4. Write the Java code that validates your user's input before you convert it to an `int`. You can assume that the user entered a positive number. The `String` variable named `response` contains the input.

_____

_____

_____

_____

LAB 8-3: VALIDATING USER INPUT

In this lab, you use what you have learned about validating input to add validation to the program you wrote in Lab 8-2. The program should validate that the user entered a numeric value when he or she makes a choice from the menu before you convert the input from a `String` to an `int`. Re-read the description of Lab 8-2 before you begin and use your solution to Lab 8-2 as a starting point. You can use the example programs in this chapter as a guide.

1. Open your source code file named `Menu.java` using Notepad or the text editor of your choice.
2. Save the program as `Menu2.java` and change the name of the class in the code to `Menu2`. You may also have to change comments that you included in your original program.
3. Add the code that validates the user input.
4. Save this source code file in a directory of your choice, and then make that directory your working directory.
5. Compile the source code file, `Menu2.java`.
6. Execute the program using the following as input:
   a. two, 1 Fries, 1 Lemonade
   b. one, 2 Fries
   c. Nothing, Choose 4 (End Order) from the menu
   d 1 Hot Dog, 2 Lemonade
   e. 2 Fries, 1 Hot Dog, why

■ ■ ■ ■ ■INDEX

Special Characters
> (greater than symbol), 28, 29
< (less than symbol), 28, 29
() (parentheses), 5, 18, 38
{}(curly braces), 4
!= (exclamation point, equal sign),
  28, 29
! (exclamation point), 29, 30
% (percent sign), 18
&& (double ampersand), 29, 30
* (asterisk), 18, 70
++ (double plus sign), 48–49
+ (plus sign), 18
-- (double minus sign), 48–49
- (minus sign), 18
// (double slash), 20
/ (slash), 18
== (double equal sign), 28, 29
= (equal sign), 18
>= (greater than or equal to
  symbol), 28, 29
<= (less than or equal to symbol),
  28, 29
|| (double pipe), 29, 30
; (semicolon), 17

A

addition operator (+), 18
algorithms, 94
ampersand, double (&&), AND
  operator, 29, 30, 41–42
AND operator (&&), 29, 30
  multiple comparisons, 41–42
applets, 2
appletviewer, 2
applications, 2
  console, 111
  standalone
    enterprise, 2
arguments, 116
arithmetic operators, 15–16

arrays, 81–92
  accessing elements, 84–85
  declaring, 82–83
  initializing, 83–84
  multidimensional, 103–106
  parallel, 89–92
  searching for exact matches, 86–88
  staying within bounds, 85
  subscripts, 82
  two-dimensional, 103–104
assignment operators, 16–17, 18
associativity, 18
asterisk (*)
  import statements, 70
  multiplication operator, 18
attributes, 3

B

block statements, 32–33
Boolean comparison, 05–50
Boolean data type, 12
Boolean operators, 28–30
  logical, 29–30
  relational, 28–29
bubble sorts, 96–103
  finishup() module, 101
  housekeeping() module, 97–99
  sortscores() module, 99–101
  switchvalues() module,
    99–101
byte data type, 12
bytecode, 7
bytecode interpreter, 2

C

case sensitivity, 12
char data type, 12
class(es), 3
  importing, 22, 70

class keyword, 4
cleanup() module, 117
comments, 20–21
compareTo method, 31–32
comparing String variables, 30–32
compiler, 2
consistency of data, validating, 123
console applications, 111
control break programs, single-level,
  73–79
counters, controlling while loops,
  52–53
curly braces ({}), 4

D

data ranges, validating input, 121–122
data types, 12–13
  validating input, 118–124
data values, swapping, 94–96
decision statements, 32–41
  if else statement, 35–36
  if statement, 32–33
multiple comparisons, 41–45
nested if statements, 38–39
declaring
  arrays, 82–83
  variables, 13–14
decorating, 71
decrement operator (--), 48–49
definite loops, 59
division operator (/), 18
do while loops, 61–63
downloading Java 2 Platform, 3

E

encapsulation, 3
enterprise applications, standalone, 2
EOF marker, 71, 72
equal sign (=), assignment operator, 18

equal to operator (==), 28, 29
`equals()` method, 30
events, 56
  controlling `while` loops, 56–57
exact matches
  searching arrays for, 86–88
  testing data for, 129
exceptions, 75
exclamation point (!)
  NOT operator, 29, 30
exclamation point, equal sign (!=)
  not equal to operator, 28, 29

F

fields, 70
files, opening, 71
`finishup()` module, 101
`float` data type, 12
flow of control, 32
`for` loops, 59–61

G

graphical user interfaces, 111
greater than operator (>), 28, 29
greater than or equal to operator (>=),
  28, 29

H

headers, 5
`housekeeping()` module, 97–99

I

`if else` statement, 35–36
`if` statements, 32–33
  nested, 38–39
importing
  classes, 22, 70
  packages, 70

increment operator (++), 48–49
infinite loops, 50
initializing
  arrays, 83–84
  variables, 14
input files, reading data, 71–72
instances, 3
instantiation, 3
`int` data type, 12
interactive programs, 108
intermediate code, 7
interpreters, 8
invoking methods, 3

J

Java 2 Platform, downloading, 3
Java Development Cycle, 6–9
  compiling programs, 7–8
  executing programs, 8
  writing source code, 6–7
Java program(s)
  structure, 4–5
  types, 2
Java programming language, 2
Java Virtual Machine (JVM), 8

K

keywords, 4, 12

L

less than operator (<), 28, 29
less than or equal to operator (<=),
  28, 29
lines, 71
logic errors, 33
logical operators, 29–30
`long` data type, 12
loop(s)
  accumulating totals in loops, 65–68

definite, 59
`do while`, 61–63
`for`, 59–61
infinite, 50
nesting, 63–65
reading data using loops and EOF, 72
`while`. *See* `while` loops
loop body, 05–50
loop control variable, 50
`looping()` module, 113–117
lvalues, 48

M

machine code, 7
`main()` method, 4–5
menu programs, 108
  writing. *See* writing menu programs
messages, 3
methods, 3
minus sign (-)
  subtraction operator, 18
  unary operator, 18
minus sign, double (--), decrement
  operator, 48–49
multidimensional arrays, 103–106
multiple comparisons, decision
  statements, 41–45
multiplication operator (*), 18

N

names, variables, 12
nested `if` statements, 38–39
nesting loops, 63–65
newline character, 71
not equal to operator (!=), 28, 29
NOT operator (!), 29, 30
null statement, 33, 50
null string, 123
null value, references, 83

O

object(s), 3
object-oriented programming, 3
opening files, 71
operations, precedence, 18
operators, 15–20
　arithmetic, 15–16
　assignment, 16–17
　Boolean, 28–30
　logical, 29–30
　relational, 28–29
OR operator (ll), 29, 30
　multiple comparisons, 42
order of operations, 18

P

packages, 2, 70
　importing, 70
parallel arrays, 89–92
parentheses (())
　`if` keyword, 38
　methods, 5
parentheses operator (()), 18
pipe, double (ll), OR operator, 29, 30, 42
platform independence, 7
plus sign (+)
　addition operator, 18
　unary operator, 18
plus sign, double (++), increment operator, 48–49
postfix form, 48
precedence, 18
prefix form, 48
priming reads, 56–57
primitive data type, 12
programs. *See also* Java program(s)
　interactive, 108
　menu, 108
`public` keyword, 4

R

reading data
　from input files, 71–72
　using loops and EOF, 72
`readline()` method, 71–72
real time, 108
reasonableness of data, validating, 123
records, 70
references, 83
　null value, 83
relational operators, 28–29

S

searching arrays for exact matches, 86–88
semicolon (;), 17
sentinel values, 50
　controlling `while` loops, 54
sequential statements, 21–25
servlets, 2
`short` data type, 12
`showInputDialog()` method, 66–67
single-level control break programs, 73–79
slash (/), division operator, 18
slash, double (//), comments, 20
sorting data
　bubble sorts. *See* bubble sorts
　rationale, 94
`sortscores()` module, 99–101
source code, 6–7
standalone enterprise applications, 2
`startup()` module, 112–113
`static` keyword, 5
string(s), 13
string constants, 5
`String` objects, 5
`String` variables, comparing, 30–32

T

totals, accumulating in loops, 65–68
truncation, 116
two-dimensional arrays, 103–104
type casts, 116

U

unary operator (-,+), 18

V

validating input, 108, 118–124
　data ranges, 121–122
　data types, 119–121
　presence of data, 123
　reasonableness and consistency of data, 123
　testing for exact matches, 129
variables, 12–13
　declaring, 13–14
　initializing, 14
　Java data types, 12–13
　names, 12

W

Web servers, 2
Web-based applications, 2
`while` loops, 50–59
　controlling with counters, 52
　controlling with events, 56–57
　controlling with sentinel values, 54
writing menu programs, 111–118
　`cleanup()` module, 117
　`looping()` module, 113–117
　`startup()` module, 112–113

subscripts, arrays, 82
subtraction operator (-), 18
swapping data values, 94–96
`switch` statement, 108–111
`switchvalues()` module, 99–101
syntax errors, 7